The
Healing
Workbook

THE HEALING WORKBOOK

Amanda Marples has asserted her right to be identified as the author of this work in accordance with sections 77 and 78 of the Copyright, Designs and Patents Act 1988.

Peer reviewed by Mayvrill Freeston-Roberts, BACP Accredited and Registered Counsellor and Psychotherapists

An Hachette UK Company
www.hachette.co.uk

Vie Books, an imprint of Summersdale Publishers Ltd
Part of Octopus Publishing Group Limited
Carmelite House
50 Victoria Embankment
LONDON
EC4Y 0DZ
UK

www.summersdale.com

Printed and bound in China

ISBN: 978-1-80007-768-3

Substantial discounts on bulk quantities of Summersdale books are available to corporations, professional associations and other organizations. For details contact general enquiries: telephone: +44 (0) 1243 771107 or email: enquiries@summersdale.com.

The Healing Workbook

Tips and Guided Exercises
to Help Overcome Trauma

AMANDA MARPLES

Disclaimer

Contents

Introduction

Picking up this book is an enormous act of courage. If you have experienced any kind of trauma, suffering or upheaval in your life, the idea of trying to heal from it can be frightening and inevitably involves a level of risk. The pain of trauma is a known quantity, but the prospect of recovery can feel strangely threatening and uncertain. What if you try to heal and it doesn't work? Wouldn't failure be worse? Maybe. But acknowledging your need to heal also reveals a belief in your ability to heal.

Trauma may have reached into every corner of your life, colouring every experience, relationship and choice. You may have spent years avoiding triggering places and situations, causing you to miss out on opportunities for joy and growth. Perhaps you feel confused and unsure of who you are any more. By starting the process of healing, you can open up your life to more authentic relationships and a more wholehearted way of living, while having a better handle on any intrusive memories.

Drawing on cognitive behavioural methods, holistic therapies and spiritual wisdom, *The Healing Workbook* is a gentle starting point to help you understand and deal with your trauma. Through a range of practical tips and exercises, you will have the tools you need to embark on your personal journey toward inner healing. You will find support and encouragement to begin to look for your lost pieces, to grieve and to find your way back to yourself, your values and a life worth living.

What this book will do for you

Your journey toward healing from trauma will be as unique as you are. That means there is no easy fix or shortcut to recovery. It will require time, work and patience. Just reading that might make you feel frustrated. It's an understandable reaction. Why should you spend time and work on trauma that you didn't ask for, didn't want, didn't cause? The answer is because you deserve better. And if you don't do the work, who will? No one else can walk this path except you.

Although it may be daunting, your healing journey can bring many positive aspects to your life. While you can never change the reality of what happened to you – or erase its impact – this book will give you valuable, everyday skills, space to explore who you are, and re-engagement with the kind of life that you want to lead.

You are going to gain insight into how trauma functions and a fresh perspective on the parts of you that are affected. You will find a range of resources including further avenues of support to explore when you feel ready. You will learn how to ground yourself using a range of techniques and practical suggestions, and with committed practice you will become skilled at regulating your emotional state.

Most importantly, this book will offer hope and inspiration that healing is absolutely within reach and help you start to take back control of your life with authenticity, confidence and the wisdom that comes from having walked a difficult path.

How to use this book

This is a workbook. The exercises suggested will help you explore new ways of thinking, behaving and being. They are the most important parts of the book. You can read through the book first if you prefer, but healing is not a passive process. **Doing** the exercises is where change begins. If you want things to *be* different, you have to *do* things differently.

You can work alone, with a friend/relative or with a therapist. Have extra paper handy and use pencil, not pen! Alternatively, use a separate notebook to write your answers. You can try the exercises several times with a different focus, if you wish, and monitor your progress on page 150.

The chapters follow a logical order, so please read them in succession. It is recommended that you learn the grounding strategies on pages 74–77 first, before you do any exercises. The work required to heal can be triggering, so knowing how to ground yourself is a wise investment of your time. Although efforts have been made to avoid obvious triggers, this is a book about trauma. You may find some parts of it tough. Words or ideas that are comparatively neutral might be distressing for you. Feel free to redact the text or replace it with more comfortable substitutes.

Finally, please take your time. You will not accelerate the healing process by working fast. Take plenty of breaks, and always seek support if you feel unsafe. Go at your own pace, with the knowledge that every step you take is a sign of your increasing courage and strength.

Part 1:
Trauma, Healing and You

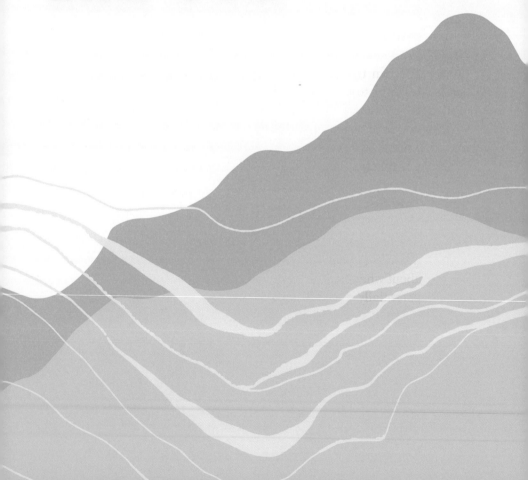

Imagine you are learning to drive. You've never driven before and you only have a vague idea of how cars actually work. Understanding is your first job. It's much less scary if you know where that weird sound came from, or why the car jolted forward like that. All cars have their quirks. Some cars have a sticky clutch or struggle on hills. You will need to know how to get the best out of it, so the journey is smooth.

You can think of your healing journey as being like learning to drive. The car is your brain, mind and body, as an integrated whole. Understanding why it behaves the way it does will help you to stay calm when learning a new manoeuvre and to know how to respond to unexpected scenarios.

This first chapter will teach you the fundamentals of your system and how trauma affects it. You will learn about the terminology and the accepted current theories of healing and recovery. You will start to think about what healing might look like and what this could potentially mean for your future.

What is trauma?

We have learned that trauma is not just an event… it is also the imprint left by that experience on mind, brain and body.

BESSEL VAN DER KOLK

There are hundreds of definitions and no universal agreement, but it is generally accepted that trauma is any experience where you felt powerless, threatened or afraid. Your everyday abilities to cope were overwhelmed, and the incident led to either a temporary or (in many cases) a long-lasting disruption to your ability to function. Trauma is both an event and the result of that event.

The impact of the trauma can show up at the most unexpected times. You could be watching television and the next minute your heart is pounding, or you're furious with your partner out of the blue, or you're suddenly taken with a sense of impending doom. A car horn can have you jumping out of your skin, while everyone else barely raises an eyebrow.

Perhaps you keep thinking "What's wrong with me?", but you feel it's not the right question to ask. You know in your heart that the question is not what's *wrong* with you, but what *happened* to you: it's the past, showing up in your present. It's trauma.

Trauma can happen in many ways. It can be a one-off event, such as an industrial accident or natural disaster, or it can be an ongoing set of circumstances, such as domestic violence or being bullied.

Trauma can be direct or indirect. You might have been assaulted or you might have witnessed an assault. It can happen to individuals or groups of individuals, such as families living in poverty. Entire communities can be collectively traumatized through experiences such as genocide, racism, sexism, homophobia, transphobia, ethnic cleansing or any other form of discrimination where your very identity, your right to be who you are, is under threat.

Childhood is often the site of trauma. Adverse childhood experiences (known as ACEs) can also be direct or indirect. Poverty, neglect, witnessing violence or substance abuse are all experiences that can lead to trauma as well as direct harms, such as physical, sexual or emotional abuse.

When it is prolonged or repeated, childhood trauma can lead to a pervasive disruption to your sense of self and view of reality. It may have become normal. You may have grown up with a sense of "so what?" about the things that happened to you, especially if you were silenced at the time.

Whether your trauma occurred during your childhood or adulthood, directly or indirectly, the trauma shattered your trust. The world was supposed to be safe, but now you can't be sure that it is, which leaves you open to the effects of trauma.

Types and terminology

The language of trauma can be tricky to understand. You may have heard mental health professionals say terms that sound confusing, so it is worth taking time to consider the ones most frequently used.

Simple trauma

Perhaps the most misunderstood trauma of all, simple trauma refers to trauma that is a one-off event, uncomplicated by factors such as shame or stigma. Being in an industrial accident or an earthquake would fit into this category. "Simple" in this context **does not mean that the trauma is less painful, less valid, or that recovery from it is easy or straightforward.**

Complex trauma

Complex trauma refers to any trauma that is complicated by interpersonal factors – in other words, caused by other people either directly or indirectly. Often this is prolonged and repeated. Most childhood traumas, domestic abuse, harassment or bullying would fit into this category. Trauma becomes complex whenever the traumatized person is left feeling ashamed about what happened to them. Often this happens because the person is made to feel like they were somehow responsible.

"Big T" trauma

"Big T" refers to catastrophic trauma, where your life was actually threatened (i.e. you could have died) or you *thought* you were going to die. This would include serious air and road traffic collisions, war and combat experiences, or rape. Experiencing a "Big T" trauma is more likely to lead to a diagnosis of post-traumatic stress disorder (PTSD – more on that later).

"Little t" trauma

This refers to relatively smaller, distressing incidents that are not usually life threatening. Most people will face these at some point. It encompasses things like bereavement or losing a job. As with simple trauma, "little t" traumas can still have an enormous impact on your life, but they are more likely to resolve quickly and less likely to lead to PTSD.

The Covid-19 pandemic is a good example. This global event caused both big T and little t traumas. Some of us came very close to death, either personally, or by virtue of being medical or emergency personnel. Many people faced the collapse of their business, were bereaved or isolated from friends and loved ones due to lockdown. Little t, simple traumas perhaps – but with a devastating impact. Some people will have had symptoms that resolved of their own accord, while others are still dealing with it years later.

The point bears repeating: simple traumas and little t traumas are no less valid. These terms are mainly used by clinicians and therapists to help them classify and develop appropriate treatment plans. Please remember that everyone responds differently; a lot depends on culture, resilience, background and previous trauma experiences.

> The takeaway message here is that this stuff is complicated – even the simple trauma. If you have been hurt by something or somebody and you are still suffering from the impact of that event today, your experience is valid and deserving of care and attention.

The results of trauma

The only way out is through.

ROBERT FROST

Trauma affects the body as well as the mind. You are reading this book because you are living with these effects on a daily basis, but what exactly are the symptoms of trauma? And do you need to have them all to be justified in saying, "I am traumatized"? The simple answer is no. While there are symptoms that are commonly reported, it is important to remember that we are all different; your reactions and symptoms will be unique to you. The time they take to manifest can also vary. They can arise immediately following the traumatizing event(s) or years later.

Noticing yourself and becoming aware of difficult feelings and behaviours is an important step away from avoidance. Beginning to get closer to the pain will help you move through it and out to the other side. Otherwise, we remain trapped.

Opposite is a list of the most common symptoms of trauma and associated behaviours. Tick all that you recognize. Remember that these thoughts, feelings and behaviours are not freely chosen. As you will learn in the rest of this chapter, your brain is in survival mode and has pretty much pulled off a full takeover. None of these reactions are your fault. Please take your time with this. If you feel overwhelmed, try the grounding exercises on pages 76–77 or just take a break.

Common trauma symptoms and behaviours

Physical symptoms

- ☐ Rapid pulse
- ☐ Sweating
- ☐ Bowel/bladder problems
- ☐ Numbness
- ☐ Fatigue
- ☐ Tiredness
- ☐ Unexplained aches and pains
- ☐ Sensitive startle reflex
- ☐ Agitation
- ☐ Insomnia and other sleep problems
- ☐ Shortness of breath
- ☐ Racing thoughts
- ☐ Flashbacks
- ☐ Nightmares/night terrors
- ☐ Muscle tension
- ☐ Panic attacks
- ☐ Dizziness
- ☐ Nausea

Psychological symptoms

- ☐ Detachment/dissociation (zoning out)
- ☐ Poor concentration
- ☐ Negative self-image
- ☐ Denial
- ☐ Disbelief
- ☐ Negative world view
- ☐ Confusion
- ☐ Shock
- ☐ Self-blame
- ☐ Poor motivation

Emotional symptoms

- ☐ Shame
- ☐ Depressed mood
- ☐ Irritability/moodiness
- ☐ Feeling disconnected from yourself
- ☐ Angry outbursts
- ☐ Feelings of fear or horror
- ☐ Feeling disconnected from the world

Behaviours

- ☐ Hypervigilance
- ☐ Avoidance of people, places, situations
- ☐ Stopping valued activities
- ☐ Self-harm
- ☐ Using substances (including alcohol)
- ☐ Comfort eating
- ☐ Numbing by any other means
- ☐ Seeking reassurance from others
- ☐ Avoidance of known triggers
- ☐ Being impulsive/taking risks
- ☐ Self-neglect
- ☐ Gambling
- ☐ Social withdrawal

As you read through this book, more and more might come into your conscious awareness. Bookmark this page and come back to it as necessary.

The limbic system

You are an animal – we all are. Mammals, to be precise. And as mammals, we are born with a complex and incredibly sensitive system, one that has ensured the survival of the species for millennia. It works, but the problem is it sometimes works a little too well.

Ever seen a nature programme? Think of a herd of zebras, grazing on the plains. They are calm and content. Their needs are met. All is well. Then a predator appears – let's say a lion. You know what happens next. An alarm call goes up, there's a split second as they all jerk their heads up and then the herd runs. What's going on?

There is a complex part of the mammalian brain known as the limbic system. You might have heard some people refer to it as the Lizard Brain. We've had this system forever and it has one job: to keep you alive.

When the limbic system senses danger through some kind of stimuli (often visual), it immediately releases various neurochemicals, such as adrenaline and cortisol, to make the body react very quickly, to make sure it can run away or fight the danger that it senses. Panic chemicals, if you will. You may have heard this reaction referred to as "fight, flight or freeze". These chemicals cause the heart to pump hard and fast to the muscles to maximize speed, strength and agility.

The bowel and bladder – and sometimes the stomach – are stimulated to empty. Who needs the extra weight when you're running away from a lion, right? The pores dilate, and sweat is produced to keep everything cool and efficient. The muscles tremble as they become primed. The pupils dilate, making vision brighter and more defined. Hearing sharpens. Everything sharpens. This reaction is involuntary – it can't be controlled – and it happens in no time at all. It is *lightning* fast. One minute they are grazing quietly – and then boom... that zebra is *gone*.

This is the mammalian state of red alert, courtesy of the limbic system. The system, not you, makes these decisions whether to run or fight (or if they aren't options, freeze and hope for the best). In addition, anything deemed to be unnecessary for survival literally switches off. In humans, the modern capacity to *think* is like an app we don't need. There's a lion! You don't have time to weigh up the options! Thinking literally goes offline until the limbic system is satisfied that things are safe again.

What about the zebras? Most of them (sometimes all of them if the lion is having a bad day) will survive. And once the lion has gone, the zebra limbic system clocks that things are now safe and calls off the panic chemicals. The zebras immediately return to their previous calm state, doing what zebras do: grazing, caring for young, resting with the herd. It's a brilliant system and it's why we are all here.

Hyperarousal

But – you are not a zebra. Today, we don't often run from or fight with predators. The limbic system is brilliant but outdated; it hasn't caught up with modern life and it's unable to accommodate our exciting new add-ons like language and imagination.

The limbic system is also unable to distinguish between immediate danger, or danger that occurred yesterday, danger that you witnessed happening to someone else, or danger that you are anticipating in your imagination. It explains why your heart pounds at a scary movie. It's why you sweat when you are about to make a speech. You have language to thank for that one. "Everyone is looking at me", "What if I trip?" or "I might sound stupid" are just thoughts, but they are treated like danger signals. They are lions to the brain. We need to understand this to understand trauma.

In normal circumstances, when the scary movie has finished or you've given your speech, your limbic system stops releasing the panic chemicals and you return to a calm state. Trauma is different. Imagine everyday events as packages on a conveyor belt. They trundle along, drop into a box at the end marked "past events" and are filed as memories. Very neat. But if the event is overwhelming, the brain hits a big red button and the conveyor belt stops. The package can't move forward. Meanwhile, your limbic system continues to sense danger. The package is still there, like an unexpected item in the bagging area. Everything is suspended in a state of emergency. This is what is meant by "hyperarousal".

Traumatized people struggle to relax. Hyperarousal is why you are on edge and struggle to sleep. According to your limbic system there's still danger, somewhere, and any reminder of the traumatic event may cause you to re-experience it as though it is happening now. The conveyor starts to move, but re-experiencing the trauma is just as overwhelming as the first time, so the big red button is pressed and the processing halts again. This cycle can continue until it is properly processed.

Studies show that people who experienced prolonged complex trauma (especially in childhood) have a larger than average amygdala (a region of the brain and a key player in the limbic system). Repeated activation causes it to grow, like a muscle. In a continually threatening situation, the limbic system takes precedence and the brain becomes sensitized to danger. Unfortunately, this results in a developmental trade-off. Other parts of the brain don't develop to their full potential, including the "executive function", which is needed to reason, plan ahead and organize. As far as the brain is concerned, making a shopping list is useless if there's always a lion nearby. If you are too foggy and disorganized to do "easy" tasks, like cooking or holiday planning, this could be the reason. You're not stupid, weak or useless. Your brain is just trying to keep you alive.

Fortunately, there are ways to process your trauma, which you will explore in later chapters. That's not to say that you won't ever need your limbic system again; you will. You just need one that is only triggered if there's an actual threat and not when you're sitting quietly at the hairdresser's.

Triggers

Triggers are sensory things that remind you of the traumatic event, to which your limbic system reacts. It could be anything: cloudy weather, an ambulance siren, the smell of lavender. The word "trigger" is often mistakenly used to describe anything that feels unpleasant. This can be frustrating and invalidating because, for you, a trigger is not a mild irritation. Triggers for you might cause unpredictable, overwhelming states of fear and dissociation.

You will need to learn how to manage your triggers before you start to do processing work. And before that, you need to know what yours are. If you don't have a clear idea of what your triggers are, don't worry. Use the table on the following pages to start observing and recording your triggers. Give yourself a few days for this; don't feel you have to fill it in all at once. As you develop the habit of observing yourself, you are likely to start noticing your triggers.

You are looking for the trigger itself, what effect it has (flashback, intrusive memory, weeping, etc.), how it affects your life today and how that makes you feel. It might be that airports trigger panic, so you avoid airports and can't go on holiday, which makes you feel frustrated. Maybe the taste of mint triggers flashbacks, so you struggle to brush your teeth, which makes you feel ashamed.

Trigger	Effect	Impact on life	Makes me feel...
Visual: colours, images, objects, gestures, weather			
Auditory: sounds, words, voices, songs/ music, weather			

Trigger	Effect	Impact on life	Makes me feel...
Olfactory or gustatory: perfumes/ scents, food smells/tastes, outdoor smells			
Tactile: sensations, textures, touch by others			

Trigger	Effect	Impact on life	Makes me feel...
Situational: places, scenarios			
Others			

Remember: If you start to feel overwhelmed, please stop, and if you haven't already done so, try to learn the grounding strategies on pages 74–77.

PTSD

When is trauma post-traumatic stress disorder (PTSD)? And does the difference really matter? Well, yes and no. Many of the symptoms of trauma, like the ones on page 17, are a normal response to abnormal (out of the ordinary) events. After all, who *wouldn't* be anxious or hypervigilant following an assault or a health scare? A fear-based response to a painful or frightening set of conditions is to be *expected*. It is normal to react in this way, but you still deserve to receive help or support (or the use of this workbook) to get through it.

In most cases, trauma symptoms will resolve of their own accord, or at least improve. Often, people can experience symptoms that are noticeably unpleasant, but not troublesome enough to be considered a disorder. PTSD, on the other hand, is a clinically diagnosable condition that differs from trauma in a few important ways. The difference is often one of duration and severity – in other words, how long the symptoms have been there and how badly they affect the person's life.

There are exceptions, but on the whole PTSD develops following "big T" and complex traumas. It can be diagnosed when the following symptoms are present:

◆ **Re-experienced events:** flashbacks and/or nightmares

◆ **Avoidance behaviours:** using alcohol to avoid memories, avoiding certain places, keeping busy, dissociating, etc.

◆ **Hyperarousal/reactivity:** being jumpy or easily startled, hypervigilant (always on guard for danger), difficulty concentrating, etc.

◆ **Mood-related symptoms**: feelings of guilt, overwhelming sadness or anger, memory problems, etc.

Trauma and PTSD

Complex PTSD (cPTSD) is a new diagnosis, not currently recognized by all clinicians or health agencies. Essentially, where complex trauma develops into PTSD, this diagnosis can be given. cPTSD recognizes additional symptoms such as difficulty in regulating emotions and problems managing relationships.

All of these symptoms can be found in all kinds of trauma, but in PTSD they are experienced to a higher degree of intensity and cause significant impairment to functioning – in other words, serious difficulty in dealing with everyday life. Differentiating between trauma and PTSD *does* matter. While both trauma and PTSD can be treated, PTSD may require more specific, professional intervention. It *doesn't* matter in the sense that distress is distress, and any and all suffering deserves care and attention.

The description of PTSD here is not exhaustive or intended to diagnose you. The best approach, if you are worried about any of this, or think you may have undiagnosed PTSD, is to seek advice and support from a mental health professional.

Whether PTSD has developed in your case or not, the exercises and strategies in this book are designed to be gentle and supportive – not disturbing or extreme in any way. That said, we all have different thresholds. If you think a particular exercise might be overwhelming, please do not force yourself to complete it. Seek professional advice or support if you feel it would help.

Healing

You might feel anxious at this stage about the work it takes to start to process your trauma. You've spent this chapter reading about the many ways trauma can happen and the impact it can have physically as well as emotionally. You have begun to look at the reality of what that has meant for your life. But healing is absolutely possible.

Part of healing is learning to take care of yourself, to acknowledge that you are a valid, valuable human being. That in itself can be a tough ask for traumatized people. So, the best thing to do is: practise now! Do you need a break? Is there something soothing you can do for yourself? Do you need to get outside help?

One of the ironies of healing is that you must get closer to the pain in order to let it go and move forward. Does this mean dismissing your experiences? Getting over it? Pretending it never happened? No. It means careful acknowledgment of your past. It means learning the strategies necessary to let the conveyor roll that package all the way to the end of the belt. It means putting the trauma in its rightful place, so that you can be in control of your life. Perhaps most importantly, healing means asking yourself what kind of life you want to have and believing you deserve to have it.

Healing and grief

The deeper that sorrow carves into your being, the more joy you can contain.

KAHLIL GIBRAN

Healed injuries often leave scars. The pain may have gone, but the scar will remind you that things were a certain way and then they changed. The path changed.

Healing is not just about learning strategies to cope. Healing also entails grief, a period of mourning for what might have been. For what time has been lost. For what opportunities may have passed you by. There will probably be much sadness.

Take a breath, and use this page to reflect on the pathways below:

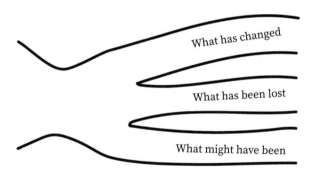

What has changed

What has been lost

What might have been

Grieving is an honourable process. Allow it. Give yourself permission to cry or be angry. Give yourself the time. Take care of yourself while it happens. You are allowed these feelings. They are valid, they are right.

Remember as you grieve that the word "recover" means to regain something lost, to take something back into one's possession. Healing is a process of recovery, of finding yourself again. Underneath the pain of trauma, you are still there.

Healing: From control to empowerment

From the mud of adversity grows the lotus of joy.

CAROLYN MARSDEN

It may feel like your life has been put on hold. Healing means moving again, sometimes in directions you didn't imagine. Healing will give you back your choices, which is not the same as control.

You're probably done with control. The control you have known so far is the kind that insists "I must not let anything bad happen to me ever again" and might have meant that your life has become very small. This kind of control makes you feel *out* of control, like a twig being pulled by a strong current.

There is a paradox for all trauma survivors. When you create safety within yourself, then you can let go of the control that you have been clinging to for safety. It's like trusting yourself to swim, instead of gripping the side of the pool. And that's when your life will start to open up. Healing, then, means empowerment.

Healing: A vision of an expanded life

Write at least three ways in which you would like your life to expand under the lotus flowers below. Write quickly, don't overthink it!

Healing and hope

Hope can be a frightening thing and can even seem dangerous. To hope is to project into an uncertain future, to proceed without knowing the outcome while feeling a mixture of expectation and wanting. "Will this work? I hope so," you might think. But there's the niggling, creeping worry that it might not, which is what makes hope so scary. Hope makes you vulnerable to disappointment and wide open to further pain. And haven't you had quite enough of that?

Nobody can guarantee anything in this life, and for you right now hope might feel too hard to engage with. There might even be a part of you that wonders if the very *act* of hoping for something will guarantee its failure. You don't want to tempt fate and have the world say, "What did you expect? You should have known better!" But if you don't have hope, what then? What is the alternative but to stay stuck?

The exercise on the next page is an exercise in hope. Think of it as a fantasy or a dream. If even that feels like a step too far, imagine you are filling this in for another person, preferably someone you know and are fond of.

If you feel able to do this directly for yourself, please look back at your losses on page 28. Think about what you might hope for in response to what you have lost. You could also look back at your quickly written lotus flowers in the last exercise (page 30).

My hopes for healing

On the bubbles, write your hopes for healing, followed by how strongly you believe this could happen for you on a scale of 0–10, where 0 is *no belief whatsoever* and 10 is *convinced this will happen*. It doesn't matter if the hopes are tiny and modest, or outrageously optimistic. You don't even have to believe any of them; just have fun with the exercise and see where it takes you.

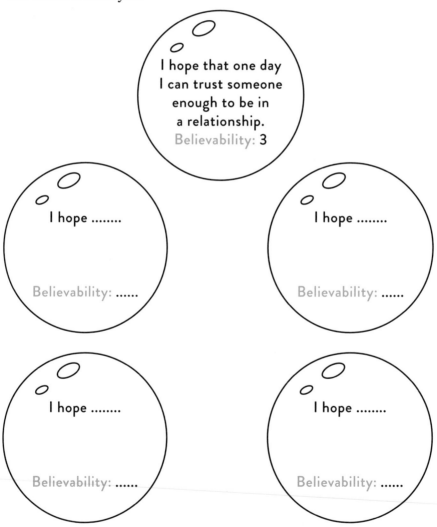

I hope that one day I can trust someone enough to be in a relationship.
Believability: 3

I hope ....
Believability: ......

I hope ....
Believability: ......

I hope ....
Believability: ......

I hope ....
Believability: ......

Part 2:
Dealing with Trauma

Hopefully by now you have a new understanding of how trauma functions and how it impacts the human system, but how do you start to heal? Let's start by imagining a tree in a back yard, struck by lightning. It's helpful to understand the physics if you want to know why and how the tree got damaged, but that won't help you to know how to return it to health.

What you need to understand first is the tree itself. What kind of tree is it and what conditions does it need to thrive? How bad is the damage? Is it something you can do yourself, or do you need to call in an expert? Just like this tree, these questions apply to you and your healing process.

This chapter is about answering those and other questions. How have you been affected by trauma? What are your patterns of thinking as a result? What do you need in order to thrive?

There are qualities you share with every other human being, but just like trees in back yards, you are also unique and have particular circumstances. Here is where you begin to tailor your own healing to fit who and where you are.

Acknowledging pain

Before you can start to heal, it is important to acknowledge that you have been hurt by something or somebody. This might be difficult. Denial is a common response to trauma because it is such an effective way to cope. Denial can come in many forms, such as minimizing what happened, i.e. "It wasn't that bad", or a literal suppression of your thoughts, which is the emotional equivalent of sticking your fingers in your ears and singing.

Sometimes other strategies are used to achieve this, such as drinking alcohol, which you will be invited to think about later. Try to forgive yourself if this sounds like you. You've been through a lot.

To acknowledge the hurt you have experienced might seem too close to acceptance. In the context of trauma, acceptance can be a hard word to accept! Accepting something seems weak, right? Or risky? Perhaps acceptance suggests that you are giving an undeserved stamp of approval to what happened?

These feelings are perfectly understandable, but for now, it's best to suspend your judgement. You will explore ideas about acceptance in more detail later, to consider how it might be a key to unlocking greater freedom in your life. In order to heal from your trauma, you have to start somewhere – by acknowledging what happened to you and how it continues to show up in your life today.

Manifestations: Acknowledging symptoms and responses

In the last chapter you noted the symptoms and feelings that you recognize. Now you will start to think about what that means for you. From the tick list on page 17, please select up to five symptoms – preferably the ones that you feel are the worst, the most difficult, the most disruptive. Then, make a note of the impact that particular symptom has had on your life, as in the following example:

Symptom	Impact
Sweating	So embarrassing. Makes me avoid people. Even friends. Have spent money on products to stop it.

When noting the impact, ask yourself: What do I no longer do as a result? What do I do to try and control it? What have I lost as a result? How does it make me feel?

Symptom and Impact

1 ....

....

....

2 ....

....

....

....

3 ....

....

....

4 ....

....

....

5 ....

....

....

Now, if you can, acknowledge the traumatic event in a few words. If you have more than one event, name the one you want to focus on first. **Don't** describe it in detail at this point. For example, "I was in a house fire" or "I was bullied for three years at work".

What happened to me:...

> **Tip:** To fully acknowledge how tough things have been, it might help to imagine this exercise has been completed by someone else. What would you say to them? What would you think?

Personal anchors

Since the trauma happened, do you feel like you don't know who you are any more? Do you sometimes wonder where the sociable, trusting person went? Or perhaps the trauma happened so early in life that you never had the chance to discover who you are. What about your dreams and aspirations? You might feel strangely awkward when someone asks what music you're into. What happened to the teenager who knew all the words and went to all the gigs? Does it feel like that person – that chance to be authentically *you* – is gone forever? Of course it does. But you have not gone anywhere. You are just blocked off by trauma. It's like you've driven into a valley and can't get a phone signal. You've just temporarily dropped out, that's all.

One way to tune back in, to reconnect, is to remember the things you love. Even if you were traumatized at an early age, there will be small things that brought you joy. It could be parmesan or plain pasta. It could be thick socks in winter or a full moon. It could be walking in the rain or your little nephew's laugh. Or Bach, cat paws, techno or stand-up comedy.

You can think of these as your personal anchors.

Please list 50 personal anchors. This may take a while, so make sure you have at least half an hour undisturbed. You might want to stop and come back to it over a couple of days. If you are really feeling stumped, use categories such as food, music, pastimes, activities, people, colours, smells, tastes, movies.

1.	2.
3.	4.
5.	6.
7.	8.
9.	10.

11.	12.
13.	14.
15.	16.
17.	18.
19.	20.
21.	22.
23.	24.
25.	26.
27.	28.
29.	30.
31.	32.
33.	34.
35.	36.
37.	38.
39.	40.
41.	42.
43.	44.
45.	46.
47.	48.
49.	50.

Keep your list safe. Treasure it. You will need to come back to it frequently.

Thoughts and feelings

Neural pathways

Imagine a thick, green forest. There are pathways in this forest that are only easy to walk down because they have been cleared by the feet of so many hikers. Everywhere else is so tangled, clearing a new path doesn't occur to you. Why would it? The thinking mind is similar to this.

Experiences and our reactions to them form connections like pathways in the brain – this is less metaphorical than you might think. Once these neural pathways form, just like forest pathways, they become the route of choice. This is how habits and associations are formed. If a child touches something sharp, a pathway forms. *Sharp thing = pain = don't touch!*

This process is how we learn and therefore how we survive, but some pathways are less useful. Think about how triggers work. That song that was on the radio at the time of the incident? The weather that day? The meal you'd just eaten? These have formed pathways. The song might be the happiest song ever written, but for you it can be a path that leads to sadness and fear. It may seem irrational, but your brain is really just doing its job. You're not doing it on purpose and you can't just turn off these reactions.

What you can do is remember that your brain is as changeable as the forest in our metaphor. New plants can grow, old trees will die; old pathways can be abandoned and new pathways can be made.

Thoughts or feelings?

Thoughts and feelings are easily confused. We are complicated creatures; we can think about feelings and have feelings about thoughts without much effort. We can even have thoughts about thoughts and feelings about feelings. It can get messy in there. That's why it's important to know the difference between your thoughts and feelings.

Consider a statement like "I feel fat". Fat is not a feeling. The feeling, or emotion, is probably shame and it arises in response to the thought. This can be hard to get your head around. The emotion feels like it comes first. But it's our perception, our thinking about the situation that produces the emotional response. We *feel* fear about something, because we *think* it is something to fear. Often that keeps us safe. But sometimes, our thinking is a little off. Sometimes we are just speculating.

Emotions are hardwired into us, they come as part of the deal. There is some debate as to how many basic emotions we possess, but most psychologists agree that there are anywhere from six to eight. Most agree that these include fear, anger, sadness, love, joy and surprise. It is thought that other emotions such as jealousy, shame and hatred, while no less powerful, are based on these. Some believe these are separate, basic emotions. It doesn't really matter. We need all of them. We need love and sadness for social bonding, and fear to avoid the dangerous animal.

But, as emotions follow thoughts, we have to learn to tell them apart. If you think something bad is going to happen (or see distressing images in your mind), which is common in trauma, you will naturally feel fear. This results in behaviour to neutralize the feeling, such as not leaving the house.

If you become aware of your thoughts, you will be more able to ask, "Is this thought really true?" You will then be able to make decisions based on how you want to live your life, rather than being at the mercy of powerful emotions that come as a result of thinking. You may have to start with the emotion initially, because they are often what we become aware of first.

In the wake of trauma, it's not unusual to have trouble identifying emotions. Most of the time you might not know how you feel or what to call it. On the opposite page is an emotion wheel. The basic emotions are at the centre, the outer layers contain the more complex or sophisticated emotions.

Over the next few days, as often as you feel able, stop, look inside and see if you can identify the emotion and the thought that may have preceded it. In the next section you will start to record these more formally, but for the next day or two just practise noticing.

The Emotion Wheel

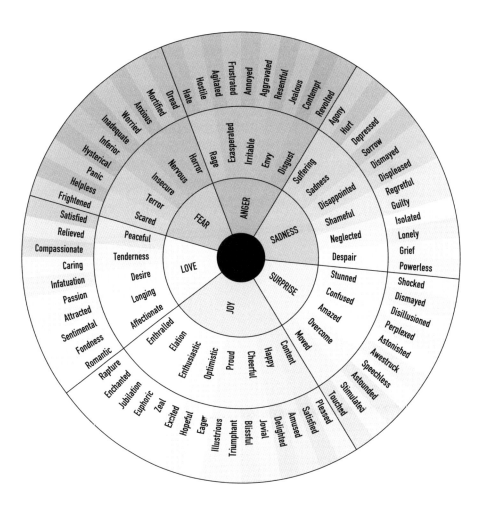

The view from here: Self-observation

Hopefully, you will have given yourself the opportunity over the past few days to start noticing your inner world, and begun to distinguish between your thoughts and emotions. This next exercise will take your increased awareness one step further, so you can gain some clarity on how trauma is affecting your life.

Over the next few days, try to write down your thoughts and emotions in the table below (or on a separate sheet of paper). You could choose to do this throughout each day or at a particular time (for instance, every morning). This exercise is purely observational. There is no need to analyze any of your observations at this point. Think of the information you record as field notes.

Please do this over at least three days (they don't have to be concurrent). A week of observations would be brilliant, but three days is good enough. Don't be tempted to skip this!

Don't worry about capturing every single emotion or thought. Just jot down what you notice, when you notice it. If you feel overwhelmed, please do take a break.

	Day 1	Day 2	Day 3
Emotions			
Thoughts			
Symptoms			

	Day 4	Day 5	Day 6	Day 7
Emotions				
Thoughts				
Symptoms				

Mindfulness

The self-observation exercise has hopefully revealed the pattern of your days. Maybe sadness slips in just after midday, or nights are when the intrusive memories come. Perhaps you often feel tired, or anger has a habit of suddenly appearing. Are you beginning to see the part your thoughts play in all this? You might have noticed the messiness and complexity of it: maybe you feel angry about feeling sad, or feel ashamed about having critical thoughts.

Whatever you discover as you work through these exercises, try to put your judgements aside and give yourself a break. Those neural pathways are so well used that the onset of emotion may be instant and overwhelming. So, how can you cope when the red mist descends, or the bottomless despair arises? You become mindful of it.* Acknowledge its presence, then approach the feeling with curiosity. You can ask yourself:

- Is this definitely a feeling or is it a thought?

- If it is a feeling, can I identify the thoughts that preceded it (including mental images, not just words)?

- Where do I feel this in my body?

- Can I describe the physical sensations?

- If I move or stretch while this emotion is here, how does it feel?

Try this for a couple of days. The more you practise, the less fearful of emotion you will be. This is excellent groundwork for challenging your thoughts.

As always, if you need a break, please take one.

*If emotions or experiences feel too overwhelming to do mindfulness in this way, please skip to grounding on pages 74–77 or self-soothing on page 101.

Skills, qualities and attributes

Part of the task of healing is reconnecting with yourself. You started this work when you looked at your personal anchors (pages 38–39); remembering what you love, the things you enjoy, and what brings comfort and peace. Here is another way to bring yourself back into focus and figure out what makes you... you.

Listing your skills or strengths (things you can do well) and your positive qualities (things about you, character traits) can help build self-esteem. The act of putting something on paper is a way of actualizing, of bringing something into being even if you don't entirely believe it to begin with. Remember, building a new neural pathway takes time and work.

Take some time now to write **at least** three things (more if possible!) under each of the following categories.

Things I am good at:

Difficult things I have overcome:

Times I have helped others:

Things I am proud of:

Things I like about myself:

Core values

Life can be confusing. We are born into the care of adults whose job it is to show us the way, to provide us with a compass with which to navigate life. Sometimes they do that well, but often they don't, or can't. Sometimes they weren't given a compass either. Even if we have been lucky enough to have had nurturing parents or guardians, most human beings have times in their life where they feel lost, adrift and wandering, with no compass. Trauma is one of those times. How can you find your compass?

Your core values are your compass. They point the way when you are feeling lost, providing a sense of meaning and purpose. Don't confuse values with goals. Goals are where you want to go, values show you the way.

Knowing what your values are can light up the path when the pain of trauma is real.

What matters to you? Connection to others? Love? Justice? Honesty? Note these around the compass below.

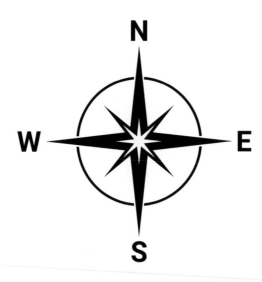

Ninetieth birthday party!
A values discovery exercise

Still struggling to name your values? Try this:

Today is your ninetieth birthday. You've had a long life and you feel rested, content and peaceful. You feel as though you have done everything you wanted to with the time you have had.

Your very closest people have thrown a party to celebrate. Everyone is here. Friends, colleagues, relatives, the guy who runs the coffee place you've gone to for years, your doctor. Everyone who knows you, everyone you know. These are all people who you trust and you have some level of affection for.

As the party winds down, people start to make speeches. One at a time, people take the mic and say a few words about you. They talk about the kind of person you are, how you have touched their lives, how they will remember you and how you have lived. In the space below, write down all the things that you would want those people to say. Not what you think they *would* say, but what you would *want* them to say. For example, you might want to hear, "You are always kind to people less fortunate" or "I can always trust you to tell me the truth".

Is that everything? Everything you could possibly want to be said about you?

Great. You just identified your values.

Mindfulness, values and acceptance

You can't stop the waves, but you can learn to surf.

JON KABAT-ZINN

If you've made it this far, well done! This is not easy work. You are looking at things that might be tough to face. But hopefully, themes and patterns will be emerging, and you will be discovering what's important to you.

Being aware of the complexities of your own pain, together with what you value, may feel like strange subjects to put together. To understand the reason behind this combination, it might help to think of a time when you had a really tough day, when it felt almost unbearable. Can you remember how you tried to cope? You may have managed well, or fought your feelings using alcohol, drugs, food or mindless television. You might have done any number of things to avoid how you felt. Of course you did. Who wouldn't? Who wants to be in pain?

But what was the cost? If you spent the day lying in bed to cope, when you value being outdoors, or if you cancelled a lunch date when you value friendship, you will likely have been left with feelings of discomfort. This is where your values come in.

Trying to avoid your feelings causes you to be out of sync with your values. To make matters worse, these bad feelings about yourself become another exhausting fight you need to have. More staying in bed, or drinking, or ignoring messages...

What if there were another way? What if you could just stop fighting? What if, instead of trying to control and even prevent the waves of pain, to stop them from coming in and crashing at the shore, you could accept that the waves are inevitable – and learn to surf?

Consider for a moment what that might look like. Try to entertain it as a possibility: by being mindful of your pain, by allowing it to be there, you might free up your energy to live the kind of life you want to live – one that aligns with your true values and your authentic self.

Any reaction to that idea is perfectly fine. It's OK to be sceptical or irritated, and you don't have to make any changes.

In the next chapters you will learn some strategies linked to this idea of acceptance and mindfulness. All that is required for now is that you hold the idea lightly in mind.

Part 3:
Looking After Your Body and Mind

Your body and mind have been through a lot together, and the road ahead is long. Before you ask yourself to do the hard work of healing, you must learn how to take care of yourself. Well-being and healing are separate things on the spectrum of human health. You cannot help but improve your well-being by beginning to heal, and improving your well-being will support and accelerate the healing process.

What is well-being? There is no universally accepted definition, but, broadly, well-being refers to your state of comfort, health and happiness, your sense of satisfaction and purpose in life. Literally, how well your state of being is.

This chapter will help you to consider some of the domains of well-being and how you can take better care of yourself. This is especially important if you want to do processing work.

There is a lot of information in this chapter to help you to start thinking about your well-being and how you might improve it. You are not being asked to make lots of changes at once and you may not feel ready to make any changes at all right now – and that is OK. If at any point you feel overwhelmed, stop, pause and breathe.

Let's begin.

Self-care

Self-care is more than exfoliating face masks, massages and ordering take-out. It's about giving yourself what you *need*, not what you want. Self-care is not self-indulgence; it means developing a Kind Inner Parent.

A kind parent puts the needs of the child right up front. Again, that's needs, not wants. The little boy might want to stay up late on a school night, but the kind parent knows that the child needs sleep and firmly but gently imposes a regular bedtime. A kind parent attends to those needs with unconditional love. They don't yell, shame or punish mistakes. "Oh dear," they might say when a drink gets spilled, "that didn't work out too well. I wonder if we could try a different way?"

This is how it must be with you, as you go forward in your healing journey. Now, more than ever, you must meet your own needs, and meet them with gentle, patient firmness. Cultivate the habit of asking yourself, "Is eating a pint of ice cream good for me right now? Is this self-care or self-indulgence?"

Sometimes you might need to go to bed instead of the party. Sometimes you will need to exercise instead of lying on the couch, or take yourself to the appointment you'd rather avoid. This is when you need your Kind Inner Parent on board to tell you, "Yes, this thing is hard. But it will be OK, you can do it and I'm with you all the way."

Exercise and green spaces

It's common knowledge that exercise is great for your mood. The release of endorphins and serotonin is linked to improved sleep, better mood, reduced stress and sharper cognitive processing – but there is more.

Recent studies show that just being in green spaces is good for your mental health. It soothes us and provides a sense of wider connection. It is also a powerful way to ground yourself, as well as an effective strategy for processing difficult thoughts and feelings. Just getting out of the house and looking around at plants and flowers, hearing the rustling of leaves, or seeing a squirrel dart across your path can give you a sense of peace and a bit of space to stand back from what's going on in your life. Solutions and insights will often bubble up during time spent outdoors. Many novelists swear by taking a walk whenever they are stuck with a plot point.

Increase your exercise and time spent outdoors as part of your healing prescription – but do it gently. You don't have to do a 10-mile hike in the wilderness or join a gym. Take the stairs. Walk daily. If you can, find a space where there are trees and grass. Any green space will do, even a city park. Sit in your local park to eat lunch whenever you can or give yourself 20 minutes to walk, cycle or simply sit. Let your mind wander and notice what happens to your inner world.

Diet

There is a huge amount of research showing the link between good diet and good mental health. Here are some basic principles to support your healing:

Eat regularly

Ever felt shaky and irritable, or yelled at someone over nothing, and then realized you were just hungry? A drop in blood sugar is the likely cause. Eating at regular times will help stabilize your blood sugar. This is especially important if you suffer from anxiety. Low blood sugar can trigger your fight-or-flight response. You start to shake and think something is wrong. Eating little and often can make a real difference to your stress and anxiety levels, so it is worth the effort.

Eat protein

Along with your other vital organs, your brain needs protein to function well. You will need your brain to be in peak condition to do the intense work needed during this healing journey. Processing, restructuring thoughts and building new pathways is very tough work. Protein also contains the essential amino acid tryptophan, which research tells us can improve mood. Protein can be found in all animal products including dairy, as well as nuts, beans, pulses and plant-based proteins such as tofu. Some research also shows that protein can combat the paralysing inability to initiate tasks often experienced by neurodiverse people. Do your brain a favour and eat protein as part of every meal.

Reduce your intake of refined sugar and saturated fats

You know this already, but the point is worth repeating. Foods that are high in refined sugars such as cakes, ice cream and some breakfast cereals have an enormous impact on your blood sugars, resulting in surges of energy followed by a "crash". Do you really need that to deal with, on top of everything else? Your Kind Inner Parent doesn't think so.

Likewise, foods that are high in saturated fats or artificial "trans fats" (found in processed foods such as take-away meals, pies or pizzas) are linked to a number of serious health problems like cancer, heart disease, diabetes and obesity. Many of us are carrying extra weight we don't need and this is also linked to mood disorders. This is not about fat-shaming or chasing some impossible body ideal. This is about giving your body the best chance of recovery you can.

Making healthy choices around your diet will support your healing. But it can be tough, especially if you have emotional or addiction issues around food and eating. You don't have to go it alone. Get support. See your doctor or a dietician. You can also check out the resources on pages 155–156 for more information about getting help if you have problems in this area.

Social media

Social media is an incredible global community, where we can connect with like-minded people, learn, access and share information at the click of a mouse. But there are clear downsides. Hashtags, likes, status updates and filters can leave us feeling anxious, excluded and dissatisfied. The habit is an addiction for many, with a detrimental impact on physical as well as mental health.

As recently as 20 years ago, we would only hear a terrible news story on the evening news, hours after the event. Now, it's livestreamed to your phone. You might as well *be* there, for all your brain knows. Remember how it can't differentiate between things happening to you or someone else? Live news can be a source of further trauma.

As humans, we have never had such unfettered access to other people's thoughts. The whole world can seem hateful, angry and judgemental. Human nature hasn't declined, it's just that we can literally see and read the passing thoughts of millions of people. We aren't supposed to! In real-life interactions, the presence of others is a strong modifier. We are unlikely to comment openly on someone's terrible haircut, questionable life choices or sketchy politics. Online is different – it's anonymous and detached. We can be mean and critical without any consequences.

The negative impact of social media is clear and backed up by research. We feel like comparative failures. We think we are missing out and messing up. The more connected we become, the more isolated and lonely we feel.

Social media: What can you do?

The social media genie is not going back in the bottle, that's for sure. This means that the power to take back control lies with you. If you feel your social media usage is out of control, or is damaging your mental health, then it's time to take action. Here are some options:

* Call a moratorium. Halt your notifications, block certain websites, delete some apps, ban yourself from the news. Give yourself time and space in the non-digital world. You can always install things again later.

* Put boundaries in place. Unplug after 8 p.m. or whatever feels realistic. Set timers.

* Get help. If you think you are seriously addicted, or your usage is making your life a misery, seek support. There are a growing number of resources to help you and you are not alone (see pages 155–156). Smartphone addiction is a real thing.

* Radical change. Downgrade to a brick! Basic phones are making a comeback and you might just change the quality of your life. Give it some thought.

You might be concerned about the potential void that could be left behind. Consider what might be fun to do instead of being in front of a screen. Drawing? Origami? Visiting a museum? Baking? Taking up a sport?

Use the lightbulbs on the following page to note some alternative activities. You could go back to your personal anchors on page 38–39 for inspiration.

Can you do it today? If not, when?

Sleep hygiene

Getting enough rest is essential to healing and for good mental health generally. But it's not always easy. You might be the kind of person who can fall asleep anywhere, but if you are struggling with trauma you are likely to have problems in this area.

Your level of healthy sleeping behaviours and patterns is known as sleep hygiene. Building good sleep hygiene practices will help you to get back on track and improve your overall functioning. Try to adopt the following principles as much as you can:

* Have regular times for going to bed and getting up, to help you to feel rested and more stable. If your schedule is erratic, you will feel erratic.

* Don't compensate! Daytime napping or sleeping in late to catch up on lost sleep will only confuse your body. Regardless of when you fell asleep or how many times you woke in the night, get up at the same time. Be stubborn about this; if you stick to regular times, your body is more likely to fall into line.

* Avoid or reduce your caffeine intake. This includes coffee, tea and chocolate. If you can, avoid caffeine after midday.

* Avoid screens for at least an hour before bedtime. No television, no phones, no laptop, no gaming. Screens are confusing and overstimulating for the brain and not conducive to producing the kind of brain waves needed for sleep. Reading or listening to music are better options.

* Your bedroom should be a sacred space, as free as possible from the associations of your waking life. Think about your sleeping environment. Consider temperature and comfort. You may need a fan, a window open or an extra blanket. What about light? Do you need blackout blinds or would a night light bring the comfort you need to nod off?

* Try not to use your sleeping area for work or hobbies.

- Develop a wind-down routine. This can create a feeling of safety, familiarity and comfort, as well as provide a cue for your body and brain that it is time to settle down for rest. This is a really simple way to put some structure into your life. Your wind-down routine can be a reliable, solid safety net to finish your day, regardless of how the day has gone.

Take some time now to think about what you would like your wind-down routine to include, highlighting from the list below as well as adding anything else that you would like, in line with the principles above.

Bath/shower Reading
Moisturizing Guided meditation
Non-caffeinated drink Yoga
Journaling Mindfulness
Music Self-massage
Planning tomorrow Stretching
Burning incense

Unhealthy coping strategies

Switching off from the pain of trauma may be a well-worn path for you. You may have been using some very effective coping strategies for a long time as a shortcut to relax, numb pain or even to dull the sensation of *being*. Perhaps you turn to drinking, smoking, using drugs, gambling, scrolling endlessly, buying clothes you don't need, disappearing in relationships or comfort eating.

You may feel justified in taking this approach: "I'm not doing anything that anyone else isn't doing," you might think – and you're absolutely right. Millions of other people are doing the same. But too much of these avoidance tactics can store up problems for the future, including your health, relationships and sense of self. Numbing will delay your recovery. Your problems are still there the morning after, regardless. You know this.

Think about what's right for *you*. What does your Kind Inner Parent have to say about these avoidance habits? What do your values say?

Healing relies on you being present. This means using tools like grounding and mindfulness to allow you to feel the present moment, to be fully *with* yourself. The next page provides space for you to record your behaviour. Please take a few days to do this – a week would be ideal, but just do as much as you feel able.

Risky strategies – self-assessment

Acknowledging your coping strategies and avoidance habits is not about judgement or criticism. It is about being conscious of your behaviour. It's just information – and information is power. Once you become conscious, you will know if it is time to do something about it, with the help of your Kind Inner Parent.

The most common coping strategies are listed opposite, but be honest: what else are you doing to take the super-highway to escape yourself? Note how many times you use any of these strategies (use a simple tally to give you an idea). If you can, also note what was going on for you at the time (bored, lonely, anxious, stressed, etc.).

Strategy	Monday	Tuesday	Wednesday	Thursday	Friday	Saturday	Sunday	Total
Alcohol								
Number of units/drinks								
Why?								
Drugs (illicit or overuse of prescribed)								
Number of occurrences								
Why?								
Overeating								
Number of occurrences								
Why?								
Screen time								
Number of hours								
Why?								

Connecting and contributing

Humans need purpose. Connecting and contributing to the people and community around you can provide it. If people feel too risky, you may choose to disconnect instead, which means missing out on being valued, hearing different perspectives, getting feedback and feeling part of something. We need the safety and comfort that the tribe can bring. If you haven't found yours yet, it isn't too late to look. Here are some ideas for reconnection:

- Send a postcard or a letter to someone you haven't seen in a while. In the age of quickly dashed off emails and texts, receiving a written note can be a very welcome thing.

- Smile at someone. Most people smile back, so be brave and try it. See what happens to your mood.

- Say hi to your neighbour and ask how their day is going.

- Join a walking group, book club or creative writing group. A quick Google or a look in your local newspaper will help you see what's on.

- Invite a friend for lunch or a walk in your local area.

Studies show that social contribution supports well-being. It is values-based, can provide a sense of accomplishment and boost your self-esteem. Options include:

- Recycling

- Litter picking

- Volunteering (if you have time and energy)

- Donating to charity, book exchanges or food banks

- Giving blood (if you are able)

- Giving up your seat on public transport, if you are able

- Participating in a carpool

Keeping it simple

You don't have to change everything in your life immediately to improve your well-being and you don't have to do anything you don't feel ready for. You have plenty of time. Life has no expectations of you. Pause. Breathe.

Lifestyle changes are hard! They take time and repeated effort. For now, you could take one action from each section of this chapter, as listed below. Complete the following sentences and remember it doesn't matter how small the action is.

1 **Exercise and green spaces** – I will ....
....

2 **Diet** – I will ....
....

3 **Social media** – I will ....
....

4 **Sleep hygiene** – I will ....
....

5 **Unhealthy coping strategies** – I will ....
....

6 **Connecting and contributing** – I will ....
....

Choose one thing from the list that you can try today or tomorrow. If you feel paralysed or worried about choosing the "right" thing, remember that "freeze" is also a trauma response. Spend 5 minutes grounding, then come back. You can even close your eyes and stick a pin in the page. Trauma makes you believe that every decision is critical. It isn't. What you choose does not matter. What matters is that you choose.

Part 4:
How to Take Control

Imagine finding a beautiful vase at a junk store. It's grimy, cracked in places, the paint is chipped, a piece is missing. It looks like it might have been used to store dirty paintbrushes, not fresh flowers. Maybe it was dropped carelessly or thrown deliberately. You look at the damage. It makes you feel a little sad; such a delicate thing deserved better treatment. But you can see its potential, and with some care and attention it can be restored. Despite the damage, it remains, fundamentally, a beautiful vase.

This is what trauma did to you. You are not the trauma. Fundamentally, you are still there. In the last chapter you began to look at how the damage shows up in your life, and your tendencies to withdraw or blame yourself, or project anger out into the world. It may still be difficult to distinguish these symptoms from your essential self. Don't worry, you'll get there.

Kintsugi is the Japanese art of repairing broken pottery with gold. The damage is highlighted, rather than disguised, to honour and value the history of the object. What it went through, what it endured. The end result is often more exquisite than the original.

This chapter will help you to begin the processing work (if you feel ready), as one part of the larger project of loving, respectful self-restoration.

Avoidance

You wouldn't be human if you didn't try to avoid pain. It's how you survived. Try to remember this the next time you find yourself shutting down when an intrusive memory or intense emotion arises. As we have learned, your brain does not know the difference between an actual event and a flashback. Your brain is just trying to keep you safe, that's all. Try not to blame yourself. Now for the *but...*

Trauma memories *do* need to be processed in order to become normal memories. Normal memories don't intrude in full, glorious technicolour. Normal memories sit in the file marked "stuff that once happened". Trauma memories, on the other hand, are yet to be filed. They are in the pending box and they keep popping up like annoying notifications, reminding you that there is work outstanding, interrupting the flow of other activities you want to be doing, like working, enjoying your hobbies or visiting friends.

The more you try to shut them down, the more insistent they get, pleading for your attention. Have you ever seen a child who wants something? They interrupt, tug on clothing or arms, or whine. If they continue to be ignored, the child is likely to ramp it up, misbehave and cause chaos, until the adult has no choice but to say, "OK, what do you want?", by which time everyone is stressed and possibly feeling a little guilty.

Think of a traumatic memory in the same way. Until you pay attention to it and process that memory sitting in your pending tray (or stuck on the conveyor), it will continue to send notifications, nag at you, cause chaos in your life and pull you further and further away from the things you would rather be doing. Your trauma memory has one purpose only – to get itself processed.

Thus, avoidance, while a completely normal and understandable reaction to distress, is only a short-term fix, a sticking plaster. Sooner or later, you have to pay attention if you want to move forward. Before you go on, please remember some key things:

- You are brave for facing your trauma.

- Restoration is possible.

- Thoughts, feelings and memories cannot harm you. They are just signals thrown up by your brain. Just electrical impulses, nothing more. The only power they have is the power we give them.

- If you are safely in the present, it is safe to look at the past.

That said, please remember that it is OK not to feel ready to do the processing work right now. If you are committed to your own healing, the right time will come. You will be invited to assess your readiness over the next pages.

Processing your trauma: Readiness

The next few pages will give you a method of processing your trauma memory. You do **not** have to do this if you do not feel ready. Some apprehension is normal, but if it feels wrong don't do it. The questions below will help you think it over.

When not to proceed

* Are you currently undergoing treatment or therapy?

* Do you have thoughts or urges to harm yourself?

* Are you diagnosed with a mental health condition OR are you worried that you may have one?

* Are your circumstances *currently* traumatic?

* Are you drinking or using drugs on a regular basis or dependently?

If you answered **yes** to any of the above questions, please seek the guidance of a mental health professional or doctor (or therapist if you have one) *before* proceeding with the work, and see page 132 for further advice.

When to go ahead

* Are you well practised and confident in your use of grounding skills (pages 74–77)?

* Are you otherwise well?

* Do you have support?

* Are you prepared to seek help or advice if necessary?

* Are you free from thoughts of self-harm?

* Do you have a sense of readiness?

* If you have answered **yes** to at least four of these questions, you are ready.

Don't be disheartened if now is not the right time; simply miss out the exercises on pages 78–79 and pick up again on page 80. It's OK not to be ready. You have not failed and you will still be healing by working through the other exercises in the book. Bookmark this page to reassess where you are.

Important: If you are not ready to do the processing work, please learn the grounding skills on the following four pages anyway. These are completely safe to learn and will support your ability to cope with any overwhelming emotion, and to regulate yourself.

Grounding skills

Avoiding your triggers isn't healing.
Healing happens when you're triggered,
and you're able to move through
the pain... to a different ending.

VIENNA PHARAON

Yes, the trauma must be faced. Memories in and of themselves can cause no harm, but it is possible that in the midst of strong emotion or a reliving experience, you may be at risk of doing things that would not be good for you. Your concentration might be affected or you might be less aware of your surroundings. You might make rash decisions you haven't thought through. You may have thoughts of harming yourself.*

Grounding is a set of techniques to help stabilize and regulate your emotional state. It is an essential skill of healing. Remember how the brain can't tell the difference between real and perceived, because our imaginations and language skills are so incredible? Grounding is a way to help the brain understand that we are right here, right now and not back there, back then; to keep you anchored in the present.

Please practise as often as you can. Find the ones that work best for you. Practise them when you are calm – don't wait until you are triggered or dissociated. You'll find it very difficult to remain calm enough to recall what you need to do, unless you are well versed in this skill. It is recommended that you do not move on to the processing work until you feel confident that you can do grounding on cue.

*If you feel at risk of self-harm at any point please see page 132 and seek help immediately.

Grounding exercises

The rules

Before you proceed, remember:

- **Always** do grounding with your eyes open. Your brain needs evidence that you are right here, right now.

- Practise as often as possible. You need to be able to do this on cue!

- Don't give up! If one technique doesn't work, keep trying alternatives until you are back on the ground. What works for some doesn't work for others. What worked yesterday might not work today. Be open to experimenting.

- Use grounding whenever you feel overwhelmed or unsafe, are reliving a memory/having a flashback, or experiencing any powerful emotion including anger. It can also be used to manage cravings for substances or other unhealthy behaviours.

- Grounding is a coping not a processing skill. Think of it like dealing with a spillage. The immediate concern is to mop it up, not to think about how it happened.

On the next page is a table of different ways to do grounding. There are dozens of ways beyond what is suggested here, so feel free to come up with your own, or research alternatives. Be open to finding what works for you and make a note of what you have tried.

> **Tip:** The bigger the trigger, the bigger the strategy. If you are reliving a memory and are in full-on fight-or-flight mode, maybe don't go for a soothing strategy! Better to do 10 minutes of star jumps (if you are able) or have a cold shower. Combine more than one strategy to max out the effect – play a word game while stretching, stroke a pet while reciting a poem. The possibilities are endless. Find what works.

My grounding skill sheet

PHYSICAL GROUNDING	My Notes
Brisk walking or jogging	
Star jumps	
Wave your arms in the air	
Stretch	
Run cold water over your hands, splash some on your face/take a cold shower	
Wrap yourself in a blanket (pressure can help you to feel located)	
Taste or smell something strong – sour lemon, chilli, strong mints, lavender, boiled sweets (good for when you are out in public!)	
Carry a grounding object – a textured stone or crystal that you can hold/feel	
Rub any rough or textured surface – zips and jewellery, or velcro can work well, and can be used in public discreetly	
If seated – hold on to the arms or seat of the chair and push your feet into the floor, your rear into the seat	

MENTAL GROUNDING (can be useful when out in public)	My Notes
Say a present-focused statement: "My name is ......, the date today is ......, I am in [location] and I am safe right now"	
Arithmetic games – count backward from a random three-figure number in multiples of seven or eight	
Category games – name a city, country, sports team, first name or occupation for every letter of the alphabet	
Describe wherever you are, without judgement: "I am in my lounge, there are two windows, the walls are green..."	
Describe an activity as you are doing it – such as making a sandwich: "I am getting out the bread, I am buttering a slice, I am looking for the salad..."	
SOOTHING GROUNDING	My Notes
Focus on favourites: photos, colours, songs, music, poems, scents – use personal anchors (page 38–39)	
Spend time with pets if you have them	
Take a bath	
Self-massage	

Trauma narrative: Part one

Here is a method to process what happened. This involves writing, preferably longhand if possible (i.e. not typed), so you will need plenty of paper and pens/pencils. Choose a time when you will not be disturbed and when you are feeling relatively calm. You will need no more than 2 hours.

Before you start, plan an activity for when you have finished writing for today. Physical exercise is strongly advised, such as a walk. Also look at your personal anchors. Plan something enjoyable. Then take a moment to check in and reassure yourself that you are safely anchored in the present. Ready?

* Write down exactly what happened, starting at the very beginning. Use the past tense (i.e. "I looked at the wall", **not** "I look at the wall").

* Use short sentences: "It was a hot day. There was a lot of traffic. ... was on the radio."

* Include as much detail as possible: the weather, who was there, what you saw, heard, felt, tasted, smelled.

* Avoid emotional or judgemental language. Approach this like a report.

* If there are gaps in your memory, do some research. Ask others who were there (**not** perpetrators of violence/abuse), look at news stories or reports.

* If you feel triggered or overwhelmed, **stop**. Ground yourself.

Continue for as long as you are able. Write to the end, leaving nothing out. It could take one or several sessions. Don't rush this. Thoroughness is always better than speed.

> **Note:** If you have multiple unrelated traumas, do one at a time. If your trauma was prolonged, either tell it in chronological order or deal with individual specific memories.

Trauma narrative: Part two

You have faced and recorded quite possibly the most painful thing that has ever happened to you. This alone is an incredible accomplishment. But now what? The next stage is for your processing to go deeper.

Again, choosing a stretch of undisturbed time, go over your work and double-check you have included every detail that you can remember. If something else comes to you, put it in. Next:

- Write the whole thing out again.

- When you are satisfied that the story is as complete as possible, read it out loud.

- If you feel triggered or overwhelmed, **stop**. Ground yourself. Go back to the beginning.

- Repeat until you can get to the end without stopping. Be patient with yourself.

- Aim to do this every day, for as long as feels comfortable.

- When you can read to the end, record yourself reading the whole thing.

- Listen to the recording. Listen again. Listen until you are bored of hearing it. That's a good sign!

- You could also read it to someone trustworthy who will listen without judgement.

Make sure you are taking excellent care of yourself while you are doing this work. Eat well, rest, hydrate and avoid mood-altering substances including alcohol.

Tell a trusted person that you are doing this work. Have them check in with you at agreed times. You might want to share your signs of being triggered or dissociated and your best grounding strategies, so they can remind you what they are.

Acceptance

Pain is inevitable. Suffering is optional.

HARUKI MURAKAMI

Your trauma story has been told. Let's say for now, it's in a file marked "the past". But just like an injury that has healed, there are scars. Anything that has once been damaged will carry some vulnerable spots.

You may find that you still have a certain level of hypervigilance, discomfort in certain situations, with certain people. You may be highly empathic and feel things very deeply. Here we come back to acceptance. In part 2, you allowed yourself to consider it, even if you found the idea difficult.

You might be thinking, "What has acceptance got to do with healing?" Look at Murakami's quote at the top of this page. It's a quote often attributed to Buddhist teaching and you can see why. Many spiritual and faith traditions teach that accepting the inevitability of pain is a path to emotional and spiritual freedom. Acceptance is allowing things to be how they are, especially when you can't change them. Fighting what you cannot change only causes suffering.

Acceptance doesn't mean tolerating bad behaviour or ignoring a problem. It doesn't even have to mean forgiveness. Acceptance means not fighting what *is*. Your boss **is** unpleasant. Sadness **still** comes to visit. Your hard work **is** going unnoticed. Acceptance allows you to be still and to choose how you'd like to respond. There is freedom in acceptance.

Acceptance and mindfulness

Accepting means making space. It means noticing your emotions and the thoughts that give rise to them with a sense of curious detachment:

"I notice I am having the thought that I am lazy."

"I notice anger is here."

"I am experiencing sadness."

Feel the emotion in its entirety then do... nothing. You don't have to change it, agree with it, like it, escape it or act it out. It can just be there, while you focus your energies on what you value most.

This might make you angry. Why should you accept something painful, frightening or unjust? Aren't you letting them get away with it? Isn't that giving in? No! The aim is to free yourself from the battle so you can think calmly and clearly about what actions you need to take, if any.

You might find it helpful to imagine your thoughts and emotions as something you can watch, like clouds passing through the sky. There are different ways to do this well-known practice. Some people imagine sitting by the side of a road, and their thoughts and emotions are the cars passing by. The idea is to observe your thoughts and emotions, without getting involved with them.

Learning to accept and make space for thoughts and emotions is a great skill to develop as you move through the early stages of processing the trauma and beyond, so do try to practise this when you can. If you feel overwhelmed or triggered, go back to grounding.

Defusion

Mindfulness is a skill that needs practice. In the early days of healing, you might find it almost impossible to do. If you find that you just cannot detach enough to observe your thoughts and emotions as clouds, or cars passing by, don't force it.

It is likely that you are fused with your thoughts and the intensity of the associated emotion makes it very hard to disengage using the mindfulness approach alone. Mindfulness as a practice has been around for centuries, but even the most serene Zen master will have days when it's just not happening. Fortunately, there's an alternative.

Defusion strategies are highly effective, light-hearted ways to detach from particularly nasty or persistent thoughts, especially the self-critical kind. Defusion means literally to de-fuse – to get a little separation between you and the thought. With defusion, you are uncoupling from the thought, not the emotion – but in doing so, there will be a positive knock-on effect on the intensity of the emotion. Defusion takes the sting out of the thought.

Please try some of the suggestions on the opposite page and have a play around with some of the ideas. Like grounding, some will work better than others for you. Have fun with them!

Defusion strategies

Whenever a thought is bothering you (e.g. "I'm a failure") write it down and then apply one of the following defusion techniques. There is space to note your findings.

Satiation

Set a timer for 1 minute and say the thought repeatedly, as fast as feels comfortable. Usually, by the end of the minute, the meaning will start to break down to nothing but a jumble of sounds.

Notes:

....

....

....

....

....

Personification

Give your internal critical voice a name or a character, to separate it from yourself.

It might help to choose something with a slightly comic ring to it. Maybe a character from your favourite comedy show, or a cartoon character, but "Bob" or "Janet" can work just as well. Then, imagine them saying the thought in a funny voice and remind yourself, "That's just Bob doing his thing. Thanks for that, Bob!"

Notes:

....

....

....

....

Sing

Sing the thought to a tune you know. "Happy Birthday" is always a popular choice. Sing it high, sing it low, sing it opera style, sing it punk rock!

Notes:

....

....

....

....

Important: These strategies are not intended to belittle or invalidate your experience of yourself, neither is the aim to eliminate painful thoughts and feelings. The goal is to get a bit of distance from them, so that *you* and not they are in control, to give you your choices back, to enable you to get on with living.

Thought challenging

Cognitions (thoughts) are natural brain events that occur almost continually, often flashing through the mind so quickly we don't notice them. You know how suddenly you feel sad or uncomfortable and you have no idea why? Often the reason is a cognition that you weren't entirely aware of, passing through and leaving an emotional calling card.

And then there are the cognitions we know about. The dark thoughts, the criticism, the worries. Don't they just totally seem like cast-iron, irrefutable facts as they echo in your head? There is literally no doubt in your mind. But all cognitions can be challenged. Think of them as opinions generated by your brain. And aren't all opinions open to debate?

If you have got this far with the workbook, you will be developing a powerful, curious internal observer. You will be getting better at noticing your cognitions. The exercise on the next page will help you to gently challenge those negative cognitions that you are noticing. Of course, some of your cognitions might turn out to be facts. That's alright. The aim is to encourage you to remain open to the possibility that your brain's opinion could be wrong, or at least not compelling enough to take notice of!

Thought challenging: Weighing up the evidence

For this exercise, choose a thought and approach it with curiosity to find evidence for and against. Please rate your strength of belief before and after. An example has been completed for you.

Cognition: *I'm no good at anything*
How much I believe this on a 0–10 scale (0 = not at all): 8

Evidence for:	Evidence against:
I failed an essay once	I passed in the end
I messed up my last relationship	I have two close friends
I can't do mindfulness for more than a minute	I can do the defusion thing
Rob is my age and has a better salary	I make a mean chilli
	I'm actually quite good at pool

Balanced conclusion: *OK I'm not terrible at everything. I still make mistakes but there are things I am good at, and I am willing to learn.*

How much do I believe the original cognition now? 3

Cognition:

How much I believe this on a 0–10 scale (0 = not at all):

Evidence for: Evidence against:

Balanced conclusion:

How much I believe the original cognition now:

Cognition:

How much I believe this on a 0–10 scale (0 = not at all):

Evidence for: Evidence against:

Balanced conclusion:

How much I believe the original cognition now:

Affirmations

Every thought we think
is creating our future.

LOUISE HAY

Let's go back to the mind as a forest metaphor. Remember those well-worn, automatic neural pathways in the brain? You may recall that once a pathway is formed, you can go from the smell of roses to full-blown flashback in an instant. But this ability can be a blessing in disguise. What sets us apart from the rest of the animal kingdom is our complex language and this is what supports the construction of these pathways in such a powerful way. We have the ability to think "I can't do it" when we see a new challenge and this sets up a new pathway with very little effort. We can build new pathways using exactly the same tools. This is how affirmations work.

Affirmations are positive statements that we repeat, to take us in the direction of the reality we want to be in. It requires more persistence to build a positive pathway using affirmations than it does to form a negative one from a frightening experience. They lack the intense, visceral, biochemical effect of pain or fear. A thought that is merely pleasant has a more neutral effect on the body.

Affirmations can feel silly, embarrassing or uncomfortable. Try them anyway, over a prolonged period. Persist with them for at least a week. They are thoughts, like any other. In the end, they will leave a trace just the same. Here are some suggestions to work with. Pick one or two. You might want to say them out loud or write them ten times in a notebook every day. There is also space to create your own.

I am a good person

Life is full of joy and opportunity

I am healing

I love myself unconditionally

I allow myself to grieve

I accept all my emotions

I always have choices

I attract healthy, loving
people into my life

I welcome new experiences

I give myself love, gentleness
and compassion

I am allowed to have needs

I release what is not in my control

I deserve good things in my life

Everything I need is within me

The past can no longer hurt me

I do not fear change

I create a space for joy

I am doing the best I can
with what I have

I have a right to say no

I am proud of who I am

I am worthy of love

Part 5:
Managing Your Healing Journey

Healing is less about the destination than it is about the journey. Your growth and your healing will be lifelong. There will always be new things to learn and new depths to discover.

It is tempting to imagine that one golden day in the future you will be perfectly fixed. If we are honest with ourselves, this is a belief most of us have. But the truth is, that future day will not arrive because your life doesn't exist in the future. Your life is today.

It may feel daunting, even disappointing, to realize and then accept that healing is a continual, non-linear process that does not happen overnight or at a single point in time. But go with it. Learning the strategies set out in this chapter will equip you to deal with what lies ahead. Healing requires prolonged, deliberate work. Mindful work. You will need to practise, until it becomes integrated into your daily routine.

This chapter will help you to think about how to manage your ongoing healing with self-compassion, to troubleshoot the sticky areas and stumbling blocks that can typically arise when doing this work.

Managing expectations

Expectations are resentments under construction.

ANNE LAMOTT

Remember the time you had to have a difficult conversation with a friend, partner, parent? The one you carefully rehearsed, covering all possible bases? How annoying is it when they don't stick to the script? Or what about the event you'd been looking forward to that looked so different in your mind's eye? How about the way you thought life would look and feel by a certain age – and it's turned out nothing like that? We all do it.

It's tough to be open to life, to let it be as it is, to allow it to unfold. It's not your fault. All mammals are designed to assess the future and to always err on the side of caution. A rabbit will leap away at the sound of wind rustling the grass, when there is no fox present. Better to be safe than sorry, is the mammalian mantra. But as humans, we also have the capacity for imagining the future in a way no other creature has. The rabbit worries about the fox right now. We worry about future foxes. We just can't help it. In the same way, we put enormous pressure on ourselves by projecting into a perfect future, telling ourselves the way things *should* be, including our own reactions and behaviours. When reality fails to meet our expectations, we can react with anger, disappointment and bitter resentment.

Research tells us that, overall, humans are actually bad at predicting outcomes accurately – a phenomenon known as "prediction errors". We also know that these errors (i.e. unrealistic expectations) are generally bad for our mental health. When things don't turn out the way we thought they would, we can become frustrated, exhausted, full of self-criticism, prone to giving up and reverting to old patterns.

A good example is dieting. The dieter begins with an unrealistic picture of themselves, perhaps super-thin or bulked-up. They often become angry with themselves for not getting there (or not getting there quickly enough), get disheartened, abandon the diet and return to former habits. The problem here is not the diet. The problem is unrealistic expectations, too high standards and too much pressure altogether.

This tendency might always be there, but there is a middle way. If you can stay aware and stay conscious of your expectations, you put yourself in a more powerful position. You can examine these future-focused ideals for signs of fantasy or flaws and be overt with yourself: "This might not go the way I imagine." This is not pessimism. Reducing unrealistic expectations will help you to let go of worry about the future, to deal more calmly with problems that do arise and to be open to the lessons that life has for you.

Setting parameters

Bottom lines

Goals for your healing journey are important. You may be an aficionado goal-setter, the kind of person who relishes the chance to make lists, spreadsheets and colour-coded planners. On the other hand, goals at this early stage might feel overwhelming, or you might not have any thoughts right now about what your objectives might be. If this is true for you, try setting bottom lines.

Your bottom line is your bare minimum. Things that as long as you do (or don't do), you can consider your day a success. Perhaps your bottom line is to speak to one person every day. It could be not to hurt yourself or not to get drunk. "No matter what," you might say, "I will not stay in bed all day to avoid my feelings." Your inner perfectionist might tell you it's not enough, but the point is to make your healing journey achievable day to day. Because some days will be tough. Some days the minimum will be all you can do and that's alright.

List your bottom lines in the space below:

No matter what, I will...

◆

◆

◆

◆

No matter what, I will not...

◆

◆

◆

◆

Top lines

Some days are inevitably better than others; you feel stronger in yourself and you will be able to do more. This is where top lines come in. Don't confuse these with goals. Top lines are your aspirations – healthy recovery behaviours that you do if you can, when you can.

Some examples might be taking exercise, cooking healthy meals, mindfulness practice or journaling. Please list your top lines in the space below. Go back to your values on pages 48–49 and your personal anchors on pages 38–39 if you are struggling for ideas.

On a good day I will...

-
-
-
-

Having clear bottom lines and top lines can help you to avoid setting unrealistic expectations around what you can do and reduce your chances of feeling overwhelmed. Bottom lines and top lines give you a space to aim for somewhere in the middle. A day in the middle is a day well spent.

> **Tip:** It can be helpful to think in terms of the day ahead. Setting goals and parameters just for today is far more attainable than thinking you have to meet your bottom lines every day for the rest of your life. Remember, we only ever have the present moment, despite our ability to imagine the future and recall the past. "Today, I can meet my bottom line. Today, I can take care of myself."

Mistakes and perfectionism

Everybody makes mistakes; they are intrinsic to the human experience. Intellectually you know this is true, but it can be difficult to tolerate and accept this idea as it relates to yourself, especially if you are struggling with trauma. Complex trauma experiences in particular might have instilled the idea in you that mistakes are not only unacceptable, but catastrophic.

In this regard, the internet is not helpful. Often the message is that we must be fit, wealthy, interesting, smart, hilariously funny and have thousands of followers just to be acceptable. Notifications and updates regularly remind us about the perfect lives not just of celebrities but of ordinary people. We compare ourselves unfairly, forgetting that much of what we see has been carefully filtered and curated. We feel compelled to compete. At the same time, mistakes are met with incredibly harsh public condemnation. It's unsurprising that we feel we must be perfect and never make mistakes.

Before going on, take some time to answer these questions, to bring into view your attitudes and responses toward this subject.

1   How do you feel about mistakes?

2   How do you treat yourself after you make a mistake?

3   What, if any, lengths do you go to in order to make things perfect?

4   Why?

Managing toxic perfectionism

Perfectionism is not intrinsically bad. Some expressions of perfectionism are healthy and represent a striving for excellence, like saying "I want to do a great job" with joy and enthusiasm. Perfectionism becomes problematic when its primary function is the frantic avoidance of failure; where there is no pleasure in the task, only fear of getting it wrong. We might call this toxic perfectionism.

Toxic perfectionism allows no margin for error. It says, "If you screw this report up, you'll look like an idiot. You'd better work on it all night without a break." It tells you that mistakes mean you are a failure. Not the work, but *you*. The fear of failure can lead you to abandon projects or turn down opportunities. Toxic perfectionism can transform an unimportant task into a distant, unreachable peak.

The answers you gave in the last exercise should help you to see if you have a tendency toward this thinking style, which includes your approach to healing. Maybe you believe your flashbacks should have stopped by now, or that you must learn the techniques by heart. Maybe you haven't even been able to try yet. To alleviate this habit, you can:

- Notice it. Toxic perfectionism often shows up in thoughts of *should, ought* and *must*.

- Use defusion techniques (pages 83–84).

- Allow your perfectionistic thoughts. Remember you do not have to act on them.

- Use grounding techniques if you feel overwhelmed (pages 74–77).

- When you are calm, set gentle, achievable bottom and top lines (pages 94–95).

Uncertainty

When you become comfortable with
uncertainty, infinite possibilities
open up in your life.

ECKHART TOLLE

However severe your trauma was, it's likely that you have been left with a strong feeling of uncertainty and worry about future events. Of course you have, this is entirely reasonable. Trauma can shatter your sense of trust in the world, your sense of safety.

When you have started to face what happened to you – and even after you have processed the memory – you may always be more attuned to the possibilities of what can go wrong. As you have learned, this future-oriented overassessment of danger is what has kept humans safe.

But just like a faulty car alarm that regularly wakes up the whole neighbourhood, your system will alert you to all possibilities of danger, often in the form of endlessly circular worry, even when everything is OK.

Life will always be uncertain. Nobody knows the future and life has a habit of taking us in directions we hadn't anticipated. There's no getting away from this. Trying to control all the outcomes is like trying to control the waves. While you might retreat to a place where you feel safe, you could also be missing out on what life has to offer.

It might be time to start to free yourself from worry, from the tyrannical dictates of the "what-ifs".

Coping with uncertainty and worry

Use the following guide whenever you feel stuck with worry. On the next page is a worry tree based on these principles.

Step 1: Identify – real or hypothetical?

Real worries are the ones actually happening: "I have run out of petrol", "My co-worker is acting inappropriately", "I have lost my wallet". Hypothetical worries are the ones that have not happened, the what-ifs: "What if nobody speaks to me at the party?", "What if I'm not home when the parcel comes?", "What if the pain never goes away?"

Step 2: Troubleshoot

If the worry is real, what can you do? Write a list of possible solutions.
   If the worry is hypothetical, go to Step 4!

Step 3: Actions

If there is something you can do to solve the problem... do it!

Step 4: Acknowledge and redirect

If there are no solutions right now, or you have done what you can and the worry is still bothering you:

* Notice it. Remind yourself you've done all you can. Remember the thought can just be there. You don't have to engage with it. Use defusion techniques if needs be (pages 83–84).

* Redirect your attention, externally if possible. For example, spend a few minutes in mindful awareness of the sky, or focus on the meal you are cooking or the tea you are drinking. Grab your personal anchors (pages 38–39) and connect to something you value. Ground yourself (pages 74–77).

* If the worry pops back up (and let's face it, it will), go back to the first bullet point in this list.

Worry tree

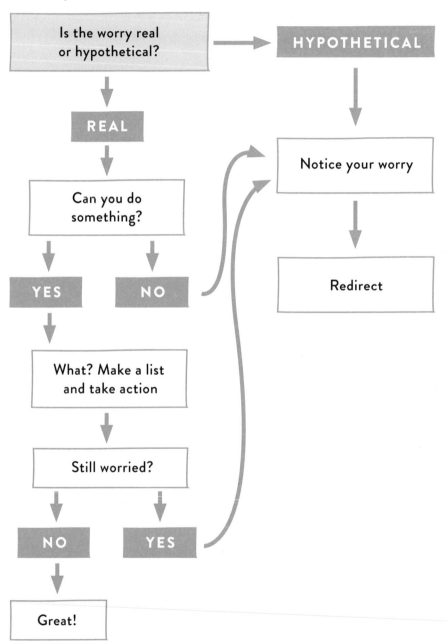

Self-soothing kit

No matter how hard you work on your recovery, there will be days when all you want to do is curl up and hide. It is natural on these days to reach for the old destructive habits: eat badly, drink alcohol or spend money to cope. But the urge to curl up and hide may be exactly what you need. You do not always have to be moving forward. You are allowed to stand still.

One way to support yourself to do this in a healthy, self-nurturing way is to create a self-soothing kit. Think of it as a first aid kit for difficult days.

On a day when you feel well, find yourself a box. A shoebox will do, it doesn't have to be fancy (unless you want it to be). Collect together things that help you feel calm and grounded.

Here are some suggestions:

- Comforting scents/oils

- Woolly socks, a soft toy, hand cream, fidget toys

- Sachets of herbal tea/hot chocolate

- Favourite music or meditations

- Photographs of loved ones or friends

- A notepad and pen

- Personal anchors list (pages 38–39)

- Affirmations such as "this will pass" or "I am safe"

- Puzzles

- A list of your bottom lines (page 94)

- A brief letter of support and reassurance from your calm self

> **Tip:** Tell a trusted person that you have made a self-soothing kit. They can remind you to use it if you appear distressed.

Part 6:
Friendships and Relationships

We need each other, and that's the truth. We were not designed to be alone. Not to live alone, work alone or play alone. Trauma can damage your belief that we need others, especially if the form your trauma(s) took was interpersonal and involved other people as perpetrators of cruelty, neglect or violence. The memories of such acts can live inside you, colouring your view of the world. Who can blame you for that? It's better to be alone and safe than risk further hurt, isn't it? But without others to relate to, it can be hard to relate to yourself. Left to itself, the mind can become an echo chamber, where fears can grow out of proportion and create fertile soil for growing false beliefs.

Relationships are sites of learning – what we like, what we don't like, what is factual and what is open to interpretation. They are also sites of growth. Contact with others provides fresh perspectives, new ideas, relief from the internal noise, a place to focus your attention and a place to hear "I feel like that too". Relationships are where you find deep wells of love that you never knew were there.

This chapter will help you to start thinking about the relationships in your life. The ones that are good for you, the ones that are not and how to manage them.

Cleaning up

Self-responsibility is the core quality of the fully mature, fully functioning, self-actualizing individual.

BRIAN TRACY

After trauma, we can become highly sensitive. A throwaway remark might hurt very much. A request or an invitation turned down can send you running back to the safety of isolation. Why do people have to be so mean? Unkind? Thoughtless? Well, that's how humans are. If you are to live fully, you must learn to be responsible for your feelings when they are hurt, so that you can take appropriate, thoughtful, positive action. This can be hard to hear. How is it your responsibility when someone else has done you wrong? If this feels triggering, notice that and ground yourself. When you are ready, here is a story to help illustrate this challenging idea.

> One morning, a friend comes to visit. You're having a nice chat, being courteous and hospitable, making sure your friend is comfortable and feeling pretty good. Suddenly, in the midst of conversation, they leap up and tip the contents of your kitchen bin onto your rug. Then they leave.
>
> What on Earth? Where did that come from? Did you do something wrong? You're certainly upset and you think back quickly over the last half hour. No, no. You're sure you didn't say or do anything offensive.
>
> And then, you're furious. Here you are, standing in the middle of a mess that you didn't make and definitely didn't deserve and, meanwhile, where are they? Nowhere to be seen! You need to find them, and make them get back here and clean it up!

The trouble is, they aren't responding to calls or text messages. You're hurt and confused, so you call another friend. You get even angrier and more convinced that they should clean it up. In the meantime, there's a pile of smelly rubbish in your house. Eventually, you don't seem to have a choice. Anyway, you're sick of looking at the mess. You clean it up.

Being hurt (whether purposely or not) by another person is just like this. You have to clean up that emotional mess someone made, because the feelings are living inside your body. They are yours and you don't deserve to live in a mess.

The importance of relationships

Research shows that positive relationships are highly protective for your mental health. In fact, studies show that the more groups and communities you belong to, the less likely you are to develop serious mental health problems such as schizophrenia – and where such an illness does occur, the better your chances of recovery.

We need a sense of belonging. This urge for closeness, acceptance and community is part of our hardwired system for survival. Being part of the tribe means warmth, protection, sustenance and support. Our early ancestors knew their life depended on it and this still resonates in our system today, thousands of years later.

Trauma damages your sense of trust and often this translates as "alone is safest". But prolonged isolation, withdrawal from the ebb and flow of conversation, interaction and even touch, will eventually block out the light of recovery. Loneliness has real health consequences, as studies have shown all over the world in elderly populations. Without other people to relate to and share with, a person can be more prone to ill health, and can lose their vitality and purpose.

So now it's time to step out of the darkness of solitude and withdrawal. You don't have to rush or do anything that feels too much too soon. You just have to be open to small risks.

- "What if I joined that book club?"
- "What if I called up Alex?"
- "Could I maybe volunteer?"
- "Is it worth it?"

Yes. Yes, it is.

My connections: Self-assessment

How has trauma affected your sense of connection? The figure at the centre of both images represents you. In the spaces around you, write down the names of people, communities or groups that you are part of now and have been in the past. Think of friends and family, social or political groups, identities, sport or leisure clubs. Think back as far as you can. Add more lines if necessary. In the second image, on the following page, write down only the names of people in the groups or communities that you currently belong to.

Reflect on this...

How many of your connections have you lost as a result of trauma, because of acute anxiety, loss of confidence or loss of trust? How does that make you feel? Acknowledge your emotion around this and make space for it. Use the emotion wheel on page 43 if you need to.

Does any of this conflict with your values (pages 48–49)? Could you reconnect in some small way? Could this be a new top line (page 95)? Do you need your Kind Inner Parent on board?

It's alright if you don't feel ready. In later chapters you may want to build reconnecting into a new habit or goal. For now, keep in mind that reconnection is possible.

Boundaries

Setting boundaries is not about keeping people away, rather it is a powerful act of self-care.

MICHELLE MAROS

Taking responsibility for your feelings when they have been hurt does not mean that hurtful people should be allowed free rein in your life. Here is where boundaries come in. Boundaries are your clearly stated lines in the sand, your personal limits and rules. They include personal space, topics of conversation and levels of intimacy.

Boundaries can help you let go of difficult feelings. That doesn't make you weak, it doesn't mean the other person won. It means you can accept what happened, learn and leave it behind.

The most important thing is that *you get to choose*. It's your life, your feelings and your body that houses those feelings. What if the friend that was unkind to you offers to make amends? You *still* get to choose whether to remain friends and to what degree. You might want to take some time to think. Have they behaved like this before or was it out of character? You might decide to give them another chance or tell them the way they acted was unacceptable. Even if they are sorry, you may decide to hold back a little, not share vulnerable parts of yourself with them, not see them on your own or limit your interactions. Of course, in some circumstances you might end the relationship altogether. You will explore that later in this chapter.

My boundaries

Use the space below to start exploring boundaries that you have, or want to have, both with others and with yourself. You can also use this exercise to think about a specific person or situation.

Use the following categories to help you:

* Emotional (including disclosure and secrets, responding to your own and others' feelings)
* Social (giving away information, texting, types of events)
* Physical (personal space, hugging, level of acceptable touch)
* Sexual (kinds of, frequency, level of familiarity, no-go areas)
* Financial (spending limits, borrowing, lending)
* Political and intellectual (sharing ideas, tolerance, arguing, when to speak your truth)
* Spiritual (sharing beliefs, tolerance levels)

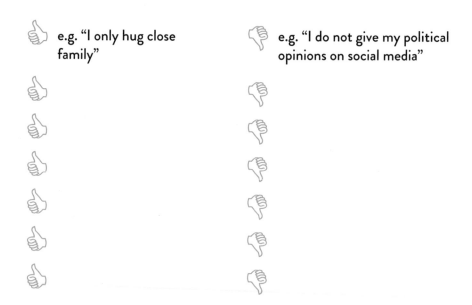

e.g. "I only hug close family"

e.g. "I do not give my political opinions on social media"

Staying safe

If your trauma was interpersonal or involved a violation by another person, then your ability to trust will have been dented, as will your ability to make a judgement. You might feel that it is better to trust nobody at all, or you might not be able to tell who is trustworthy and who is not, and often find yourself in harmful relationships. Part of healing is relearning how, and whom, to trust. You can find some key signs of trustworthy and untrustworthy people on the next page.

Everyone behaves badly on occasion, and conflict is normal in relationships. The key here is patterns and frequency. If someone *always* lies, or *frequently* belittles you, they are probably unsafe. The litmus test is how they react to criticism. The trustworthy person might say, "You're right, I was insensitive there", but if they explode in rage, try to justify their behaviour or blame you for something they did, they are probably unsafe.

Trustworthy people...	Untrustworthy people...
Listen	Have a history of being abusive
Keep a confidence	Use guilt or shame to get what they want
Are willing to look at their part in a disagreement	Never apologize, or apologize often but don't change their behaviour
Are willing to hear your side	Talk over you
Will compromise	Insult or belittle you
Never hurt you physically, sexually or emotionally	Hurt you physically, sexually or emotionally
Tell the truth in a sensitive way	Tell lies
Can admit when they are wrong	Don't admit to mistakes
Are consistent	Are unpredictable
Will apologize for mistakes and make amends appropriately	Attempt to convince you that you have misunderstood if you call them out on bad behaviour (gaslighting)
Respect your boundaries	Intrude on your space and time
Give you space if you ask for it	Leave you feeling uncertain
Have clear boundaries	Use rage or silence to punish or control you
Can hear and accept the word "no"	Play the victim
Support your choices even if they don't agree with them	Use threats

In the space below, jot down the names and contact details of people you know you can trust, using the previous page as a guide. Include professionals such as health or care personnel, lawyers and social workers, as well as family, friends, colleagues or managers.

Name:

....

Address:

....

Number:

....

Name:

....

Address:

....

Number:

....

Name:

....

Address:

....

Number:

....

Name:

....

Address:

....

Number:

....

Name:	Name:
....	....
Address:	Address:
....	....
Number:	Number:
....	....

Name:	Name:
....	....
Address:	Address:
....	....
Number:	Number:
....	....

Does the list of untrustworthy characteristics on the previous page remind you of anyone in your life right now? Part of your healing is to create safety. The boundary work you have just done can include dealing with unsafe people. Do you need to stop spending time with certain people? Do you need to end a relationship? Don't forget that family members can also be unsafe and you have a right to walk away from them too. Either way, seek support. Start with your safe list above. Reach out, so that you can talk through your options. One more key thing: violence of any kind is not OK. No amount of grounding or mindfulness will change that. The thing to do is get help *now*. See page 155 for useful resources.

Assertiveness in relationships

Before you start to think about asserting your needs and wants, you need to know what they are. Needs are similar to boundaries: they are the things that you absolutely must have in order to feel comfortable and at ease in the world. These are your deal-breakers. Wants are the things that would help, but you could manage without if necessary.

If you are recovering from trauma, you might have very specific needs. These could be simple issues like making sure you are near an exit when being seated at a restaurant, not having appointments after dark, asking friends not to tell you something distressing without warning.

Your wants on the other hand might be more flexible. While you might prefer to see a female nurse at the health clinic, you might be willing to go ahead if one is not available. More and more settings are working in a trauma-informed way and more individuals are sensitive to this too. These people – maybe even friends and family – will accommodate your needs and often your wants if you state them.

On the next page, there is a table to help you begin to make these distinctions. Don't worry if you don't have all the answers now. As you grow in awareness you will be able to add to it.

Assertiveness: My needs, my wants

In the first column, write down your main relationships and contacts. Include formal ones as well as friends and family. The middle column is your wants. What things would make these relationships easier? Maybe you prefer morning appointments, for example. Think about location, language, time, gender, boundaries and triggers. The end column is for your deal-breakers. What are your absolutes when it comes to these relationships? What is over the line? Perhaps an appointment after dark is not acceptable.

This will help you see where you can be flexible. For example, your "no after-dark appointments" rule might mean that you can go up to mid to late afternoon, even though morning is still your preference.

Come back to this table and review it from time to time, to see how your needs and wants in relationships change as you begin to heal.

Relationships	Wants	Needs

Assertiveness: Asking for my needs to be met

It's one thing to know what you need. It's another to ask for it. Asking for what you need might feel excruciating. The fear of anger and what others think of you (Selfish! Rude! Demanding!) might be a sensitive issue, perhaps wrapped up in your trauma, but you have a right to state your wants and needs. If they aren't met, consider it information to help you decide what to do next.

"The dentist won't accommodate my chaperone? I'll find one that will." Sounds easy, but in reality, it's not. How do you tell someone you're tired and want them to leave? How do you say you'd prefer to go somewhere else because this place is too noisy? And perhaps the hardest assertiveness skill of all, how do you say "no"? It might help to know what non-assertive styles look like: passive, aggressive and passive-aggressive.

Scenario: You've been invited out for dinner and the suggestion is a seafood place. You hate seafood.

Passive response: Sure. I don't mind (except you do and cancel at the last minute)

Aggressive response: You know I hate seafood. How come you always choose?

Passive-aggressive response: Well, if that's what you want. I guess I'll just have the salad.

Do you recognize yourself in any of these responses? What might an assertive response be? Let your values on pages 48–49 be your guide.

Assertive response:

Assertiveness hacks

Hack #1: Spell it out

As much as we like to believe otherwise, humans aren't very good at reading each other's minds. What makes it harder is our reliance on messages and email, which lack the essential cues such as tone, body language and context to interpret people – and we often get it wrong.

Be clear. Saying, "I'm afraid I don't have time to post your letter" is better than "I'll try my best!"

Hack #2: Buy yourself some time

Make a habit of meeting every request for your time, attention, presence, energy or your company with "I just need to check something, can I get back to you?" This gives you breathing space, to ask yourself what you really want to do, and whether it feels OK to say yes with conditions, or no.

Hack #3: Plan your exit

Friend coming over? Are they an Olympic talker? Feel burned out every time they visit? Give them a time frame: "I only have until six today." A good friend will respect that and will be prepared when you gently remind them at 5.45 p.m. that you have to wrap it up.

Hack #4: Hand guilt back

What you want and need can be difficult for someone to hear, or they can feel inconvenienced or annoyed. You do not have to engage with feelings of guilt or take responsibility for their feelings. If you have been fair, respectful and calm, you're in the clear. Allow them to have their feelings.

Saying "no"

Part of developing assertiveness skills is learning the art of saying "no". Somehow, that two-letter word can feel impossible to say. There's a good chance that you believe "no" is pointless, especially if your "no" was ignored once. "No" can also leave you vulnerable to manipulation: "If I say no to my friend, she might not want to be friends anymore." "No" can be difficult for others to hear, and you may be hypervigilant to the feelings of others and feel responsible for them. This may be part of a style of behaviour known as co-dependency, which is common among childhood trauma survivors (see resources on page 155). Being passive and agreeable might have been a survival strategy once.

"No" is loaded. But you need "no". "No" is protective, powerful. "No" says, "What I want matters."

Let's see what happens without "no". Think back to times when you went along with something (not trauma related) – the time you did a favour you had no availability for; the time you went to the museum you weren't interested in; the time you ate the cake you didn't want. Choose one scenario and fill in the flow diagram on the following page.

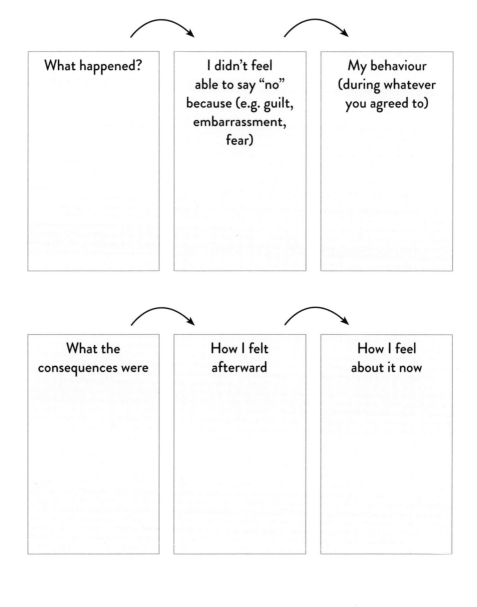

What happened?	I didn't feel able to say "no" because (e.g. guilt, embarrassment, fear)	My behaviour (during whatever you agreed to)

What the consequences were	How I felt afterward	How I feel about it now

What would you do differently? What would you advise a friend in the same situation?

Ways to say "no"

You can refuse something without saying the word "no", if it's a little too much to begin with. Here are some stock phrases to keep in your back pocket:

- "That's not going to work for me"
- "I don't think so"
- "I'm flattered but I have a partner"
- "I would rather not"

- "I am going to pass on that"
- "I'm afraid I can't do that"
- "I'm not available"
- "Thanks for the offer, but I'm good"
- "Maybe some other time"

Practise saying these with a friend, a therapist or on your own to the bathroom mirror. If "no" still feels difficult or triggering, choose a time every day when you feel calm and repeat it quickly for at least a minute, to reduce its power (remember defusion techniques on pages 83–84).

Some people will be pushy: the person who wants your number, the sales rep, the relative who thinks you should be at the family gathering. The "stuck tape" method can be effective here. Keep repeating to yourself: "I'm going to pass. I'm going to pass. I understand, but I'm going to pass."

Finally, if you have been extremely assertive, you may feel guilt or shame afterward. Be ready to enlist your Kind Inner Parent to remind you that...

- "You did a great job back there"
- "You explained very clearly"
- "You stayed calm"
- "You aren't responsible for them or their feelings"

- "If you had agreed it would have been worse"
- "These guilty thoughts and feelings are just thoughts and feelings. How about you turn your attention to something else?"

Part 7:
Staying on Track

Imagine you've had a long day at work or college and the commute was a nightmare. You get home and the house is untidy. You're already annoyed when you discover there's no milk in the fridge. You'd been hoping for a bath and an early night but now you have to go to the shop. On top of that you have a headache. By the time you've dealt with chores, pets, perhaps children, and eaten a hasty dinner, it's already late. You know you should probably go to bed but where is time for *you*? You zone out in front of the TV and eventually drag yourself to bed feeling like you're doing this healing thing all wrong. Sound familiar?

Don't worry. Remember you've come a long way and learned an enormous amount about not only a very complicated condition, but also yourself. You've picked up plenty of tools and have new resolve to take care of your body and mind. That's a lot of new stuff to integrate!

Our modern world is bristling with demanding, complicated distractions that can pull you away from your centre of gravity and leave you feeling disconnected. How on Earth can you maintain your gains in a context like this? Difficult days or weeks are inevitable. Sometimes it might feel like it's not going right. This chapter will help you find your way back.

Cultivating routines

The human brain loves routine. It also loves variety and change – this is particularly true of people who are neurodiverse. But on the whole, healthy routines that contain elements of pleasure and soothing can be anchors in the midst of a busy life, and will help you feel safe, in control and connected to yourself. Establishing routines or habits – behaviours that become so embedded in the rhythm of your life that you hardly even think about them – requires persistence in the form of repetitive action.

Studies show that it takes on average 66 days or two months to form a new habit, but the range can vary enormously from person to person. Much depends on motivation and commitment, of course, but if you can persist with something over that two-month average, chances are you'll continue with it. A couple of months is relatively quick if we consider how long some of our less healthy habits might have been with us. Sixty-six days of taking a walk after lunch, or starting each day with a downward-facing dog pose, or not taking your phone to bed at night. A couple of months... and your target habit can become almost as natural as breathing.

Over the next few pages, you will be able to identify and plan new routines to help you stay on track. Please be gentle. Making too many changes at once can be overwhelming, even triggering. One or two changes at once is enough. If in doubt, go with one.

But first... how is the weather where you are?

To stay on track with any new routine you want to build, you will need to get into the regular habit of noticing and accepting the shifting landscape of your moods. You are like the sky. Your emotions and feelings are the weather. The weather moves over the sky, darkening it with clouds or brightening it with sun. But the sky is always the sky. When checking in with your internal weather, bear in mind these truths.

The weather is as the weather is

Accept where you are right now. You can't change the weather by thinking about it. All you have to do is notice. "Today I'm sad." "Right now, I'm angry."

You can't swim in the desert, but you can sing in the rain

Do what you can. Sometimes the ground is barren and flowers will not grow. Other days you feel at your best, even in high winds and lashing rain.

Today's weather is all you need to know

Notice your weather, every day. Yesterday's snow has melted. Tomorrow's weather will happen whether you think about it or not. Stay in today as much as you can.

Write these down, along with any other affirmations you like. Keep them in your wallet, taped to your mirror or propped up on your desk at work.

My healing habits

In part 3 you started to explore some of the ways you can begin to take care of your body and mind. Use the tree to record the habits or routines you would like to build. The leaves on the tree have been labelled for ease, but don't feel you must complete them all. As you build new healthy habits that give you a renewed sense of self, hope and optimism, your old unhelpful habits are more likely to wither and fall away. Please note these on the fallen leaves.

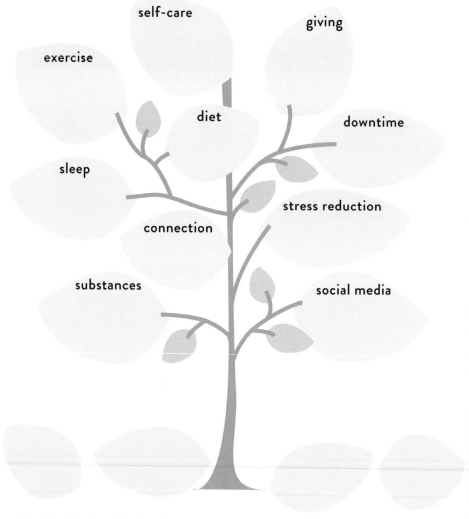

self-care

giving

exercise

diet

downtime

sleep

stress reduction

connection

substances

social media

Making it happen: My habit planner

This exercise is intended to support you to establish one new, workable habit. Drawing from the last exercise, choose a habit or routine. Start with the most appealing or the one that seems easiest. This is your desired habit. Fill in the columns on the next page, thinking carefully about how realistic this is in the context of your life. If you can't see your new habit working out, don't worry! Choose another, and remember that you have plenty of time to explore. If you begin to feel overwhelmed, step away and take a break. Go for a walk, take a few moments of mindful awareness, perhaps call upon one of your grounding strategies. When you are ready, come back to the page. An example has been given as a guide.

> **Tip:** One great way to nurture a new habit is to attach it to something that you already do routinely, such as brushing your teeth. Rather than being brand new and easy to forget, the habit will merge with an existing structure, making it more likely to succeed.

Desired habit	Reality check	Workable habit	Making it happen: my supportive actions	How will I benefit?	When will I start?
Journal every morning for an hour	I struggle with mornings and I barely have time to walk the dog as it is; I sometimes feel more positive after lunch	Journal for 15 minutes after lunch	• Buy a new gel pen • Set reminder in my phone • Wear my headphones • Put my out of office response on emails	• More connection to myself • Keeps me alert to what is going on with me • Feel good about myself	Tuesday, 5 May

Desired habit	Reality check	Workable habit	Making it happen: my supportive actions	How will I benefit?	When will I start?

Checking in

How will you know if your healing journey goes off track? The first step is being aware of your behaviour as you go through the days and weeks. Like steering an ocean liner, just a one-degree course alteration will be hardly perceptible, but over time the boat can be miles off course. In the same way, it can be hard to notice tiny slips in healing work such as forgetting to practise your techniques, missing appointments or allowing others to encroach on your time.

Regularly checking in with yourself will help you to see where small course adjustments are needed. Set up a regular time. Put it in your diary, or in your phone as a repeat appointment. How often you do this is up to you, but more than once a week may feel overwhelming and more than once every two months may be too little. Aim for somewhere in between.

On the next page you will find a check-in sheet, which includes a set of prompt questions, to guide you through a kind of self-assessment. On the next page there is an example of what your filled in sheet might look like.

Am I...	Evidence	Is an adjustment needed?
Looking after my health?	I stretched most days but missed my dental appointment	Yes, rebook my appointment
Doing valued activities?	No – too much Netflix; haven't got round to painting yet	Yes – order paint! Use habit planner
Practising new skills?	Grounded every day this week and used affirmations	No – good enough!
Respecting my own boundaries?	Turned down drinks when I was tired, but I agreed to visit Dad when I didn't feel up to it	Yes – practise assertiveness statements before calling parents in future
Doing any old unhealthy behaviours? (i.e. substances; staying up too late)	Probably using television to numb myself	Yes – practise mindfulness at least twice next week

Am I...	Evidence	Is an adjustment needed?
Looking after my health?		
Doing valued activities?		
Practising new skills?		
Respecting my own boundaries?		
Doing any old unhealthy behaviours? (i.e. substances; staying up too late)		

When things are going wrong

How do you know when things have gone from an off day to a more serious dip in your mental health? If the trauma you have experienced is not resolving, or is getting worse, then it is time to reach out for help. Here are some signs to look out for, with space below to note any personal indicators that you need extra support:

* Deterioration in sleep

* Mood that is so low you are unable to work or study

* Not taking care of the basics like eating or personal hygiene

* An increase in being triggered, accompanied by reliving experiences (flashbacks) or nightmares

* Thoughts of harming yourself or others (in which case seek urgent medical help)

Notes

Your safety and well-being are paramount, and you have come so far and worked too hard not to take that seriously. Do not hesitate to seek immediate help from a health professional, or reach out to trusted friends or family to support you to get help if you notice any of these issues. Your safe people are listed on pages 113–114.

Be reassured that traumatized people can and do recover, even if things get worse for a while. Try not to frame this as a failure on your part. You are doing the best you can with the tools you have. *The Healing Workbook* is not going anywhere and you can come back to it when you feel ready.

Off days

You promised yourself you'd go to the gym three times a week, every week, until the end of time. It started off well, you felt great: in control, upbeat, proud. And then one day you just didn't feel up to it. A stressful day, maybe a disagreement or the beginnings of a cold. It would have been fine to skip a day except your inner critic showed up right on cue, with its insidious sneaky voice: "There's no point now, I knew it was all for nothing. What a loser. Might as well go back to laying on the couch every night." You cancel your membership.

Healing from trauma can be just like that. Some days you will not want to show up. You will be overwhelmed and find yourself indulging in behaviours you thought were long gone. Your mindset here is critical. Slips happen, and a lapse is not necessarily a relapse. Having a tricky day does not mean that your hard work was for nothing or that you should abandon the emotional six-pack you're developing. Healing never happens in a straight line and – as long as you are facing the right direction – off days are nothing to fear.

Try to see a slip, or an off day, as a wrong turn on the way to your destination. Perhaps you don't know the area very well and there are unexpected diversions due to roadworks. In this scenario, would a satnav yell at you, or call you stupid and lazy? Does it say you should turn round and go back home? No. It calmly says "recalculating route".

Putting yourself first

You should sit in meditation for 20 minutes each day – unless you are too busy; then you should sit for an hour.

ZEN BUDDHIST PROVERB

The point of this Zen message is clear. If life is pulling you off centre, you will be unable to meet life with the calm capability you long for. Being frazzled and scattered leads to mistakes, resentment and burnout. This is especially true if you have caring responsibilities to children, pets or elderly relatives.

This might go uncomfortably against the grain. So many of us are taught that prioritizing ourselves is selfish or egotistical. But it makes sense. Remember that in an emergency, the advice is to apply your own oxygen mask first, otherwise, how can you be of use to anyone? It might help to think of prioritizing your healing as putting on your oxygen mask.

And more often than not, life can usually wait. Your tired, overworked mind will invariably tell you that everything is urgent, so get into the habit of pausing and asking yourself: "How important is it?" Do you really have to call the bank right now, or can you spend a few minutes with your list of personal anchors to settle and soothe yourself? Do you have to help with homework before dinner, or can you go for that run you promised yourself, which will leave you refreshed and grounded? Come to think of it, can dinner be a can of soup instead of the superfood extravaganza you had planned? Of course it can.

Part 8:
Looking Forward

You've done a lot of uphill work. The contents of this workbook may have been triggering, even annoying, in places. The work might have challenged your beliefs about yourself and the world, as well as perhaps offering you a new way to see things and new hope for your future. All of this is normal. Either way, if you have worked through some of the suggested exercises, you will have picked up lots of new skills and ideas. You may even be starting to feel some relief from the worst of your symptoms, or at least feel that you are more able to contain and soothe them.

So, now what? What comes next is integrating these ideas into your life and your future objectives, with your values firmly in mind. This might be quite enough for now and that's absolutely fine.

This chapter will help you to get in the habit of collecting positive evidence, developing a healing practice, setting goals, looking at what might be next and reviewing your progress.

Developing your healing practice

Practice might make perfect, but that's not really the point. Your healing journey is "a practice", meaning, it's how you live your life, a repeating pattern with no end point, not something you stop doing when you have mastered it, like practising a difficult piano piece for a recital.

Imagine the yoga masters. They don't stop once they can do a headstand or some other incredible feat of strength and flexibility. They continue. It is their practice. The yoga master's practice might be to stretch each night or meditate in the morning. A writer might say, "It is my practice to journal before doing any other writing." An accountant might say, "My practice is based on legal and ethical principles."

Your practice will be something you do for no other reason than because it is a good and welcome part of your life – because it strengthens, sustains and nourishes you. Your healing practice comprises the actions you take to continue your journey, in order to become more competent. Your healing practice is how you make recovery an integrated *part* of your life, in order to *have* a good life.

Preparing for therapy

At this stage of your healing journey, you might want to go deeper. You may have only looked at one aspect of your trauma(s). You may have had a taste of what kind of life might be possible and you want more. Good! You deserve the best that life has to offer.

Formal therapy might be your next step. The work of therapy will be yours and you will need to be prepared. It can be destabilizing and you can feel worse before you feel better. Therapy is also active, never passive. It's like having a personal trainer. They can tell you which weights to lift and how to lift them; they can even cheer you on. But you have to lift the weights yourself. You also wouldn't go to the gym without water, the right shoes and a decent warm-up. You wouldn't want to risk a pulled muscle.

There are steps you can take to help you prepare for therapy. Practise grounding until you are a master. Practise asking for what you need, as well as identifying and making space for emotion and difficult thoughts. The more able you are to calm your hyper-aroused system, to create a sense of safety and containment, the more you will come to trust yourself and the further you can go.

Cultivate your Kind Inner Parent and take them with you to sessions. The one that says, "Hey, it's alright. Let's just name the colours we can see. I'm holding you safe. You've got this."

What is out there?

Accessing therapy will depend a lot on where you live. Talk to your doctor or look online. Local libraries, hospitals and newspapers may also have information on what is available in your area, so it is worth checking there too. Here is an overview of the most commonly endorsed treatments for trauma.

Cognitive behavioural therapy (CBT)

An evidence-based, time-limited therapy that uses a range of techniques to effect change in thinking and behaviour. Agreed homework tasks are a critical component of treatment. Length can vary from 6 up to 26 sessions depending on complexity. CBT is commonly used for a range of anxiety and mood-based disorders such as depression, OCD, phobias and panic disorder. Trauma-focused CBT takes a phased approach that starts by achieving stability before going on to process and integrate the trauma memory. CBT is a treatment of choice for trauma according to many health bodies around the world including the World Health Organization, National Health Service (UK) and National Institute of Mental Health (US).

Dialectical behavioural therapy (DBT)

Based on the principles of CBT, with a strong emphasis on managing emotions, tolerating distress and interpersonal skills training. Often suggested for individuals with complex PTSD and/or difficulties with emotional instability. Traditionally, DBT requires attendance at both group and individual therapy.

Acceptance and commitment therapy (ACT)

Also based on the principles of CBT, ACT emphasizes living a valued life despite illness or pain. Helpful for people with lifelong or chronic difficulties including physical as well as mental health and those for whom traditional CBT has not been effective.

Eye movement desensitization and reprocessing (EMDR)

A form of exposure therapy first developed in the late 1980s by Francine Shapiro, who noticed that involuntary eye movement appeared to be associated with recalling trauma. Her original research found that bringing eye movement under a certain level of control helped to reprocess trauma memories, reducing the severity and frequency of reliving experiences (e.g. flashbacks). Therapists use various eye movement and other sensory protocols during a session. A course of treatment can be as little as six sessions, but for more complex difficulties additional sessions may be recommended.

Always go through accrediting or regulatory bodies when searching for a therapist and always check out the credentials of anyone you approach. Any reputable therapist will understand the importance of this and will *never* be offended or throw up roadblocks if you ask to see their licence to practise or registration number (depending on where you are in the world). If they do, this is a red flag and you should find someone else. Trust your intuition; if it feels wrong, don't do it!

Remember you can always change your mind. There are thousands of therapists to choose from, and now we live in the age of online meetings, your options are even broader. It is absolutely worth taking the time to find the right one for you.

Positive data logs

Changing self-limiting beliefs such as "It's impossible for me to be around other people" will take time, but it is entirely possible. One way to do this is to start a positive data log. Whenever you are about to do something that is worrying or anxiety provoking, record your thoughts and feelings about it and the strength of your belief.

You can try this using the space provided, but please do get yourself a notebook or file and continue with this work as you move forward in your recovery. It is an excellent way to use evidence from your lived experience to slowly build an upward spiral. An example has been provided:

Event	Belief	Strength of belief (%)	What happened	New belief
Dan's party	I won't cope	80%	It was hard. I was triggered and had to go outside to do grounding. I had fun overall and am glad I went.	I have tools to cope with symptoms

Event	Belief	Strength of belief (%)	What happened	New belief

Here is another way of logging evidence over time, but using your unhelpful beliefs as your starting point, and building evidence as you go.

Write your belief at the top of the page, and collect positive evidence as you go, as follows:

Belief: I will never get better
Initial strength of belief: 75%

DATE:	Evidence against:
23/4	I went to the supermarket when it was busy
28/4	I only had one flashback today
10/5	I applied for a job

Re-rated strength of belief: 70%

12/5	I'm sleeping better
15/5	A friend said I seemed more confident
20/5	Went to the christening
1/6	Attended the interview even though I was really anxious

Re-rated strength of belief: 68%

Every so often, re-rate the strength of your belief. Take care to note which way the scale goes!

This is an effective way of chipping away at a belief that is holding you back. Add to it frequently. Don't discount the small gains.

Remember that you may be prone to selective attention – that is, only noticing the things that fit with your unhelpful belief. It is an unfortunate quirk of being human, that we can receive a hundred positive comments about our new haircut, but which is the one we remember, home in on, go over in our minds? The one unpleasant comment, of course. This is the way we are. Your mind needs a leg up. Keep your positive data log ongoing and add to it whenever you receive evidence to refute your self-limiting belief.

SMART goals

To move forward, you need goals. Research shows that people who set goals are more focused, positive and likely to succeed than people who do not. But care is needed, especially in the early days of healing. Often, our goal setting is unrealistic or overwhelming. This can push you into giving up, which will chip away at your confidence.

Goals should always be SMART. For example, "I want to be better off" is great, but how are you supposed to get there? Doesn't it sound like an awful lot of pressure? Setting vague goals is like being given a destination but not a map!

SMART goals are your map. They should be:

* **S**pecific: What do you mean by better off? What does it look like? "I want to build up some savings."

* **M**easurable: How will you know this is improving? "I will make a budget and save X amount each month. I will not go over my budget."

* **A**chievable: Is it possible to get there? What can you definitely do? "I can definitely save X amount each month. By June I should have X in savings."

* **R**ealistic and **R**elevant: Think again, is it really doable? Why is this important? "X amount is doable. If I have savings, I will feel safer."

* **T**ime-Limited: How long will you do this for? Break it down if necessary. "In four months, I will have X. In eight months, I will have X. By one year, I will have enough savings to last for a month if needed."

Tip: If this is too much, stick with setting bottom lines for now (page 94).

Your SMART goals

Here's your chance to practise setting specific goals.

Phase 1: Mind dump!

What does a healed future look like? Working? Finding a partner? Living somewhere else? Coping with panic? Write down whatever you imagine in the thought bubbles. If you are stuck, go back to the work you did on values on pages 48–49.

Phase 2: Make it SMART!

Grab a pencil and notebook and choose one goal. Don't overthink it. Go with what appeals most, and work through the following prompt questions:

- **S**pecific: What will it look like exactly? Can you narrow the focus down to one thing?

- **M**easurable: How will you know you are going in the right direction? What signs will there be? What changes will you notice?

- **A**chievable: Can you really do this specific thing? Do you need to break it down even further? Do you need advice or support from someone else?

- **R**ealistic and **R**elevant: Double check – is this possible? Will anything get in the way? Why are you doing this anyway? Does it align with your values?

- **T**ime limited: How long are you giving yourself for this? Can you include some milestones?

Phase 3: Mission statement

Finish with a **mission statement**. For instance: "By the end of March next year, I will have saved enough money to put me one month ahead."

....

....

....

Tip: Talk your goal through with someone else, a therapist if you have one, a friend or other trusted person. Another perspective can help you see things you might have overlooked.

Committed actions

Goals are things you work toward and are an expression of your values. They can shift and change, and do not have to be set in stone. You may never get there, but they push you forward.

Committed actions, on the other hand, are things you do right now to move you on, and are not dictated by your emotional state. They are actions you take, regardless. Think about it. If someone says they can't come to dinner because they have a commitment elsewhere, that means they have something else they cannot say no to. They might prefer to come to dinner, but they are committed to that other thing. Likewise, committed actions are promises you make to yourself.

A committed action says, "Yes, I am sad. But I am committed to walking the dog, because caring for my dog is a value of mine." Committed actions replace the *buts* in your life, with *ands*: "I want to see my friends, but I am too anxious" becomes "I am seeing my friends and I am anxious."

You can live a valued life, despite the pain.

What committed actions can you take this week, in the service of your values? Fill in the form opposite.

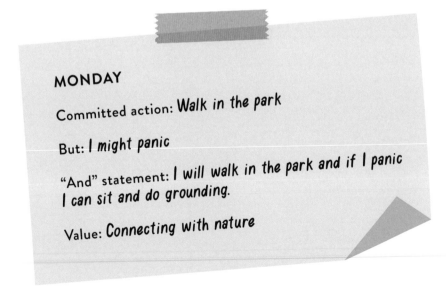

MONDAY

Committed action: Walk in the park

But: I might panic

"And" statement: I will walk in the park and if I panic I can sit and do grounding.

Value: Connecting with nature

MONDAY

Action:..................................

But: ....

"And" : ....

Value: ....

TUESDAY

Action:..................................

But: ....

"And" : ....

Value: ....

WEDNESDAY

Action:..................................

But: ....

"And" : ....

Value: ....

THURSDAY

Action:..................................

But: ....

"And" : ....

Value: ....

FRIDAY

Action:..................................

But:..................................

"And":..................................

Value: ....

SATURDAY

Action:..................................

But: ....

"And" : ....

Value: ....

SUNDAY

Action:..................................   "And":..................................

But:..................................   Value: ....

From this point in your healing journey, make regular time to look at your committed actions. Are you replacing *buts* with *ands*, or are the *buts* getting in the way of living the life you want?

Reviewing your healing practice

You can keep track of the tools and techniques here. Don't worry if you have not tried all of them.

Tool/technique	Tried?	Useful?	Make part of practice?
Acknowledging pain, page 35			
Identifying emotion, pages 40–43			
Personal anchors, pages 38–39			
Self-observation, pages 44–45			
Connecting to values, pages 48–49			
Grounding, pages 74–77			
Telling my story, pages 78–79			
Mindful acceptance, pages 80–81			
Defusion strategies, pages 83–84			
Thought challenging, pages 85–87			
Affirmations, pages 88–89			
Setting bottom/top lines, pages 94–95			

Tool/technique	Tried?	Useful?	Make part of practice?
Worry tree, page 100			
Self-soothing kit, page 101			
Setting boundaries, pages 109–110			
Habit planner, page 127			
Checking in, pages 129–131			
Positive data log, pages 142–144			
SMART goals, pages 145–147			
Committed actions, pages 148–149			

Now, fill in the following blanks to create your healing practice statement of intent. Copy it out and place it somewhere prominent!

I will include .... (insert tool) in my practice every .... (frequency) or whenever I am .... (e.g. triggered, sad) in the service of my goal(s) of ....
....
(e.g. getting a career in animal care), which is/are based on my value(s) of ....
.... (e.g. kindness to animals).

My learning

Remember when you were too scared to ride a bike without stabilizers? Remember when all of a sudden you were doing it without thinking? Did you reflect on it? Probably not! Even the smartest kid is unlikely to ask, "What have I learned about myself?" in a conscious way – but it's a question we should ask, because limiting beliefs about our capabilities can hold us back.

You can change this. Your positive data log will help, but let's ask the question right now.

What have you learned about yourself through doing this work? Finish the sentences.

Before I started this work, I always thought that I

....

....

....

Before I started this work, I never thought that I

....

....

....

I have noticed that when I think ... I automatically feel

....

....

....

The most important thing to me is

. . . .

. . . .

The most helpful thing I can do when I am hurting is

. . . .

. . . .

One of the most soothing things for me is

. . . .

. . . .

My feelings are

. . . .

. . . .

I am able to accept

. . . .

. . . .

It turns out, I am more able to ... than I thought

. . . .

. . . .

Conclusion

You made it!

Massive congratulations. This stuff is no walk in the park. Be very proud of what you have done and how brave you have been. Remember that bravery is not the absence of fear; it is doing the scary thing despite the fear. And now here you are, at the end... the end of the book, that is.

Really, your journey has just begun. There will be days when your mind insists you have learned nothing, made no progress. You will feel disheartened. But those days will come less frequently – and when they do, you have tools on board. You have a Kind Inner Parent, knowledge, strategies to manage thoughts and feelings, goals to work toward and a set of values to live by. *The Healing Workbook* has facilitated these changes, but the work is all yours. Say that again, out loud: "This work is all mine."

Healing is cyclical. You might want to do the workbook again, or you might be thinking of formal therapy. Or you may need a break, to let things settle and integrate while you consider what is next for you.

Whatever you decide, it is possible to go deeper and reach hitherto undiscovered parts of yourself. New levels of pain, perhaps, but always new levels of joy in the act of living. There will always be new frontiers, as long as you are willing and trust yourself.

Go forward, in love and great faith.

Resources

General online trauma resources

checkpointorg.com – websites and emergency numbers for most major countries/regions

complextrauma.org – resources and tools for people experiencing trauma, and their loved ones

skylight.org.nz – range of resources and support (New Zealand-based)

traumaresearchuk.org – resources and up-to-date research on trauma

Specialized online trauma resources

beyond-conflict.co.uk – remote support and counselling for survivors in conflict zones

blacktransalliance.org – information and support for Black trans and non-binary people living in London, UK, and surrounding areas

galop.org.uk – UK-based support and information for LGBTQI survivors of abuse or violence

goodmenproject.com – support and resources for men

healthline.com/health/mental-health/racial-trauma#finding-support – a resource addressing racial trauma and abuse

malesurvivor.org – support and resources for male survivors of sexual abuse

mhanational.org/racial-trauma – US-based support and information for racial trauma and abuse

nami.org/your-journey/identity-and-cultural-dimensions/LGBTQI – US-based support and information for LGBTQI community

nationaldahelpline.org.uk – UK-based domestic violence helpline

nqttcn.com/en/community-resources – US-based support and information for queer and trans people of colour

servicesaustralia.gov.au/family-and-domestic-violence – Australian-based support, information and resources for survivors of domestic violence

suicidepreventionlifeline.org/chat – suicide and crisis support with online live messaging (only available in the US and certain territories)

theara.com/resources – support and information for neurodiverse people

thehotline.org – US national domestic violence helpline

traumahelpforwomen.org – US-based peer support for women

tstresources.org – support and resources for sexual abuse survivors

veteranscrisisline.net – support for veterans

Therapeutic resources

dharmaseed.org/talks – free talks and meditations, available to download

getselfhelp.co.uk – resources and worksheets on all aspects of cognitive behavioural therapy

headspace.com – guided meditation and mindfulness (chargeable after initial free trial)

insighttimer.com – free guided meditations, available to download as an app

psychwire.com/harris/resources – variety of ACT-based resources

selfhelpfortrauma.org – trauma tapping technique (TTT)

sleepfoundation.org – resources and guidance on all sleep-related matters

youtube.com/plumvillage – channel devoted to Zen Buddhist talks and lectures

Addiction resources

aa.org – Alcoholics Anonymous, for anyone who wants to stop drinking

coda.org – Co-Dependents Anonymous, for anyone wanting to develop healthier relationships

drinkaware.co.uk – advice and support to stop or reduce drinking

eating-disorders.org.uk/international – support and information on eating disorders from the National Centre for Eating Disorders (NCFED)

focalfilter.com – free basic website blocker

freedom.to – website blocker (chargeable after initial free trial)

getcoldturkey.com – website blocker, free and chargeable versions available

internetaddictsanonymous.org – Internet and Technology Addicts Anonymous, for anyone who wants to stop compulsive internet and technology use

na.org – Narcotics Anonymous, for anyone who wants to stop using drugs of any kind

oa.org – Overeaters Anonymous, for anyone who wants to stop eating compulsively

virtual-addiction.com – resources for technology addiction from the Center for Internet and Technology Addiction

Further reading

Bessel Van Der Kolk, *The Body Keeps the Score: Mind, brain and body in the healing of trauma* (2014)

Brené Brown, *Atlas of the Heart: Mapping meaningful connection and the language of human experience* (2021)

Dannie Lu Carr, *Brilliant Assertiveness: What the most assertive people know, do and say (2012)*

Gabor Maté, *In the Realm of Hungry Ghosts: Close encounters with addiction (2009)*

Melody Beattie, *The Language of Letting Go: Daily meditations on codependency (1990)*

Paul Gilbert, *The Compassionate Mind (2010)*

Pia Mellody, *Facing Codependence: What it is, where it comes from, how it sabotages our lives* (2002)

Russ Harris, *The Happiness Trap: Stop struggling, start living (2008)*

Steven C. Hayes, with Spencer Smith, *Get Out of Your Mind and Into Your Life: The new acceptance and commitment therapy* (2005)

About the author

Amanda Marples is a social worker with 20 years' experience in community mental health, including extensive work with trauma survivors. Amanda is also a writer and has been featured in a number of publications. She is the creator of Reconcile Creative, a mentoring service for neurodiverse writers, and hopes to help level the writing and publishing playing field. This is a subject close to her heart since Amanda, her partner and two children are all neurodiverse in one way or another. It's chaos most days, but she wouldn't change it even if she could.

THE ANXIETY WORKBOOK

Anna Barnes

Paperback

978-1-80007-397-5

The Anxiety Workbook contains practical advice, effective tips and guided exercises to enable you to recognize and process your anxiety. Based on trusted techniques and mindfulness exercises, this guide will allow you to better understand your anxiety and will provide the tools you need to work through it.

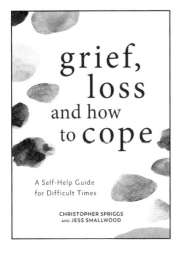

GRIEF, LOSS AND HOW TO COPE

Christopher Spriggs and Jess Smallwood

Hardback

978-1-80007-396-8

Grief can affect us at many stages in our lives – after the loss of a loved one or a job, during a divorce, or after a child has left home. With bite-sized advice and comforting words, this book is a calm and approachable guide to coping with grief and loss, which will help you navigate your feelings and find strength again.

Have you enjoyed this book?

If so, why not write a review on your favourite website?

If you're interested in finding out more about our books, find us on Facebook at Summersdale Publishers, on Twitter at @Summersdale and on Instagram at @summersdalebooks and get in touch. We'd love to hear from you!

Thanks very much for buying this Summersdale book.

www.summersdale.com